red & white
cross stitch

red & white
cross stitch

helena turvey

inspired by the

classic designs of

Toiles de Jouy,

folk art and

red and white

ceramics

hamlyn

I dedicate this book to my loving husband Raymond, who has been so supportive and invaluable to both of our families over the past few years.

First published in Great Britain in 2003 by
Hamlyn, an imprint of Octopus Publishing Group Ltd
2-4 Heron Quays, London E14 4JP

Copyright © Octopus Publishing Group Ltd 2003

ISBN 0 600 60838 7

A CIP catalogue record for this book is available from
the British Library

Printed and bound in China

10 9 8 7 6 5 4 3 2 1

Contents

Introduction

The colour red is sacred in tribal societies the world over. It is the first colour of the rainbow, the colour of the setting sun and the fire in the hearth that provides us with warmth and heat. Red sends messages to both humans and animals of strong emotions: joy, passion, anger, lust, danger, warning and attraction.

Red encompasses a variety of shades and depth of colour, from deep maroons and rich burgundy-reds to earthy, rusty terracotta and orange hues, blending into bright crimson, scarlet and vermilion, then gradually changing from magenta and cerise to the cooler shades of soft, dusty rose-reds and fading to pretty pale pinks.

Early civilizations used minerals of red and yellow ochre, grinding them to make the deep reds and orange pigments painted in their caves. Through history, and in many cases right up to the present day, such natural resources – including minerals, insects and plants – have been used to make red dyes. Vermilion, for example, was made from the mineral cinnabar, ground into a brilliant red pigment sometimes called 'dragon's blood'. Red plant dyes come from madder roots and safflower petals. The latter were used to make the bright red colour 'rouge', as well as the dye for the red tape that was tied around correspondence from solicitors and barristers.

Insect dye sources include the brilliant red kermes insects, that were once mistaken for berries as they fed off the kermes oak, an evergreen tree found in southern Europe and North Africa. Carmine-red is still made today on the Canary Islands from the cochineal insects that infect cacti, while scarlet grain is a scale insect from which a brilliant orange-red dye was made and used in Turkey and Russia.

The names of different reds come from a diverse range of (often natural) sources. The obvious one is 'rose'; a more obscure name, for a deep purple reddish-brown, is 'puce' (meaning flea in French), which was a colour much favoured by Marie Antoinette. 'Maroon' probably comes from the French 'marron', meaning chestnut, reflecting the colour of the chestnut's skin,

while 'cerise' is a light, clear red derived from the French word for cherry.

The red and white projects I have gathered together for this book use as many shades of red as possible, reflecting the style and colours of the original sources of my designs. Inspiration came from 19th-century designer William de Morgan's mythical animals, handpainted on ceramics in red lustre; Victorian tiles; books on folk art; and Toile de Jouy fabrics depicting gloriously romantic scenes involving people, distant lands, magnificent buildings, and plenty of flora and fauna. I also discovered interesting individual objects – including an unusual red and white Delft beer mug, old English ceramics, and a rare red and white Chinese Willow Pattern dish – that were perfect for translating into cross stitch embroidery. To display this broad selection of reds to best effect, most of the designs have been stitched on white, ivory, cream and very pale pink backgrounds.

All these influences have helped to make this a book of varying styles, to suit a wide range of interiors. Regardless of style, through their beautiful array of red shades, all of the projects create a warm and welcoming feel that can easily be incorporated into any home.

The projects range from simple to complex, so that some can be worked quickly while others present more of a challenge. The finished embroideries have then been applied to objects both large and small, for each room of the home. There is also a chapter for projects that make ideal accessories or special gifts.

Read Chapter 6 on Materials and Techniques before you select a design, purchase materials and start to stitch. Follow the instructions carefully and you will be rewarded by beautiful red and white embroideries that will add the perfect finishing touch to your home. I hope you will enjoy stitching the projects as much as I have enjoyed researching and designing them.

The living room

When I asked my family what their living room meant to them, they used phrases such as a meeting place and a sanctuary, and the words reflection, relaxation, warmth and cosiness. There is nothing more comforting than sitting by the fireside, close to your favourite people with your dog or cat entwined around your feet, contemplating the world or reading a good book on a cold wintry night.

Decorate your living room in warm shades of red and relax by the glowing embers of the fire. Hold back the curtains with the folk art-inspired curtain tie and look out at the stars on a clear frosty night, or lean against the soft fleecy bolster cushion, reading a good novel in the pool of soft light thrown by the Toile de Jouy lampshade. Sit by an open fire and sort through the treasures in your flower-decorated trinket box, with a cup of coffee on the pretty embroidered coffee table runner.

You can adapt all these designs to furnish your living room in different ways. Frame the William de Morgan bolster design to make an unusual picture to hang on the wall. Embroider the Swedish curtain tie motif onto a circular tablecloth, or transfer the rose design from the trinket box onto a set of linen cushions for the sofa. Use your imagination and transform your living space into a truly warm, welcoming and original room.

William de Morgan bolster cushion

The inspiration for this design came from a William de Morgan plate decorated in red lustre. De Morgan rediscovered lustre metallic glazes – a kiln-firing process used in the 9th century – by accident and then perfected the process. His plates, tiles, bowls and pots are decorated with the most fantastic mythical and delightful realistic animals, painted beautifully in red silhouettes. See page 98 in the Gifts and Accessories chapter for his charming dodo design, which I have used to decorate a plain cream apron.

measurements

Worked on 14 count Aida, the finished embroidery measures 16 x 23cm (6¼ x 9in). Use 2 strands of cotton in the needle for cross stitch and for backstitch inside the large flowerheads. Use one strand for all other backstitch and French knots. Work French knots with 3 twists around the needle.

materials

To work the embroidery:
• Piece of 14 count antique white Aida, 26cm (10¼in) wide x circumference of bolster cushion plus 3cm (1¼in)
• Stranded cotton embroidery threads as specified in the colour key
• Tapestry needle size 24 or 26

To make up the cushion:
• Medium-sized bolster cushion
• Piece of good quality red fleece fabric, 1 x 1m (39⅜ x 39⅜in)
• Red and cream sewing threads
• Basic sewing kit
• Sewing machine

▷

stranded cottons

	DMC	Anchor	Skeins
	814	45	2
	304	47	3
	350	11	1

Backstitch

	DMC	Anchor	
	154	72	1
	304	47	

French knots

	DMC	Anchor
●	154	72

to work the embroidery

Start stitching at the centre of the design and in the centre of the Aida, following the chart. To treat the finished embroidery, see page 104.

to make up the cushion

CUTTING OUT

Measure the length of the bolster cushion to the centre of each end and mark this measurement onto the wrong side of the fleece fabric, adding 12.5cm (5in) to each end for gathering. Measure the circumference of the bolster pad and add 3cm (1¼in) to give a 1.5cm (⅝in) allowance for the centre back seam. Cut out the fleece, making sure the bolster ends are cut very neatly as they will be left raw.

ASSEMBLY

On both long sides, trim the Aida to 4cm (½in) from the embroidery and turn in 1cm (⅜in) to the wrong side. Pin and tack down the long sides to neaten the edges, ready for topstitching onto the fleece.

Tack in the centre lines on the right side of the embroidery and the fleece. Position the embroidered Aida right side up on top of the fleece and lengthways across the width (bolster circumference) of the fleece, matching the tacking lines. Pin, tack and topstitch the embroidery into position on the fleece (1). Secure the raw edges of the Aida with zigzag stitch.

Place the 2 long sides of the fleece together wrong side out, to make a tube. Check that the ends of the Aida line up where they meet. Pin, tack and machine stitch the centre back seam together, leaving both ends open. Cut off loose threads, and if the seam ends are out of line trim neatly to the stitching line, as they are left raw.

Turn the fleece cover right side out and stuff the bolster cushion through one open end, placing it centrally inside the tube. There will be spare fabric at each end of the bolster.

TASSELLED TIES

Cut 2 strips of fleece for the tasselled ties, each measuring 61 x 3cm (24 x 1¼in). Cut 4 tassels, each measuring 15 x 8cm (6 x 3¼in). Leaving a gap of 2.5cm (1in) from the top of each tassel, cut strips about 1cm (¼in) wide and 5.5cm (2¼in) long from the bottom of the tassel.

With right sides out, fold each end of the 2 tassel tie strips lengthways and oversew for about 2cm (⅜in) by hand. Attach each sewn end to one side of a cut tassel on the wrong side (2).

Roll the tassel around the end of the tie, securing with a few stitches at each roll (3). Secure the last roll with a few oversewn stitches to keep the tassel together.

To finish off, tie each tasselled tie twice around the loose ends of the bolster cover close to the cushion and pull snug to gather the fabric.

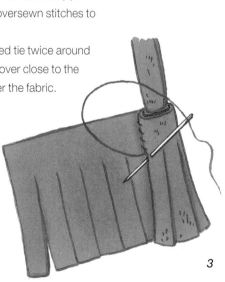

bolster cover end

measured circumference + 3cm (1⅛in)

RS   RS

3cm (1¼in)

bolster cover end

2.5cm (1in)

5.5cm (2¼in)

1cm (⅜in)

WS

WS

RS

12.5cm (5in)   measured length   12.5cm (5in)

1

2

3

Coffee table runner

The inspiration for this table runner came from an old sofaback cover, found on one of my market expeditions. The embroidery design was sewn only on one edge, in one colour and entirely in stem stitch. I thought it pretty and have adapted the idea for a table runner. The design is repeated at each end and in the centre of the cloth, and the runner is completed with white tassels at each corner. Alternatively, you could sew handmade lace onto the ends for a very attractive finish.

measurements

Worked on 14 count waste canvas, the central embroidery measures 19 x 11cm (7½ x 4¼in) and the end embroideries 20 x 10cm (8 x 4in). Use 2 strands of cotton in the needle throughout.

materials

To work the embroidery:

- Tracing paper for pattern
- Piece of white cotton/linen mix fabric, 91 x 34cm (36 x 13⅜in)
- 3 pieces of 14 count waste canvas, each 25.5 x 15cm (10 x 6in)
- 3 pieces of tear-away interfacing, each 25.5 x 15cm (10 x 6in)
- Stranded cotton embroidery threads as specified in the colour key
- Tapestry needle size 24 or 26

To make up the table runner:

- Double-knit cotton yarn, for tassels
- Piece of card, 9.5cm (3¾in) wide
- White sewing thread
- Basic sewing kit
- Sewing machine

to work the embroidery

Following the pattern diagram, make a tracing paper pattern and use it to cut out the cotton/linen fabric for the table runner. Tack in the centre lines for each piece of embroidery and mark in the seam allowances. Secure the raw edges of the fabric with zigzag stitch.

Prepare the 3 pieces of waste canvas and tack each piece into position, sandwiching the cotton/linen fabric between the waste canvas and tear-away interfacing.

Start stitching at the centre of each design and in the centre of the waste canvas, following the chart. When the stitching is complete, remove the waste canvas and interfacing (see page 100). To treat the finished embroidery, see page 104.

to make up the table runner

ASSEMBLY

Fold 0.7cm (¼in) along all raw edges of the runner to the wrong side of the fabric. Press, tack and machine stitch. This leaves a 2cm (¾in) hem

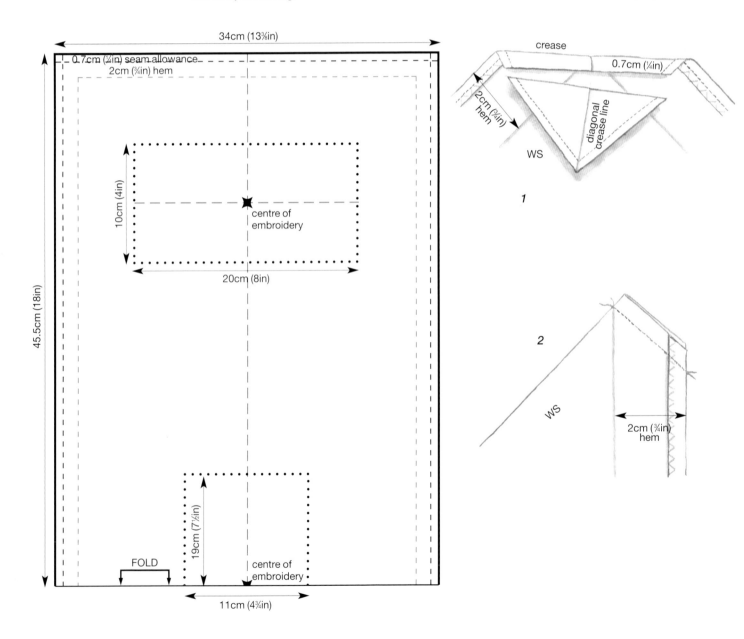

34cm (13⅜in)

0.7cm (¼in) seam allowance

2cm (¾in) hem

10cm (4in)

centre of embroidery

20cm (8in)

45.5cm (18in)

19cm (7½in)

FOLD

centre of embroidery

11cm (4¾in)

crease

0.7cm (¼in)

2cm (¾in) hem

WS

diagonal crease line

1

2

WS

2cm (¾in) hem

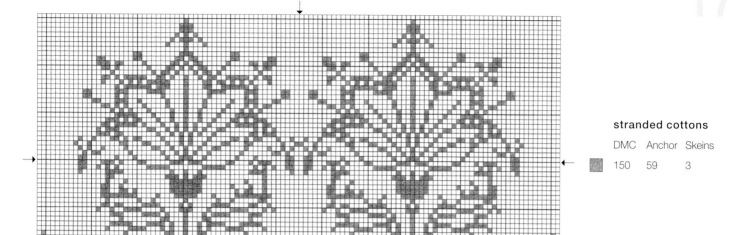

stranded cottons

	DMC	Anchor	Skeins
▨	150	59	3

allowance. Fold and press the hem allowance to the wrong side. Before stitching the hem, you need to mitre the corners.

Fold the point of each corner in half, wrong sides together, and crease. Fold in the corner point to the diagonal crease line and crease to mark this angle (1). Unfold and and cut off the corner point, leaving a 0.7cm (¼in) seam allowance. Fold the corner angle in half, right sides together, and machine stitch the 2 thicknesses together to make the mitre (2). When all the corners have been mitred, turn them right side out and pin, tack and press the mitred corners and the hem (which should be facing to the wrong side), then machine stitch close to the edge.

TASSELS

Wind the cotton yarn around the piece of card about 20 times. Catch all the threads at the top of the tassel (one edge of the card) with a threaded needle, passing it through 2 or 3 times, and pull to tighten to keep the threads together. Pull the yarn off the card and secure the top of the tassel with the needle and thread. To make the head of the tassel, wind the thread around the tassel several times to make a neck about 2.5cm (1in) from the top and pull tight. Secure the thread, push the needle up through the top of the tassel and sew it onto the corner of the runner. Repeat for the remaining 3 corners. Trim the ends of the tassels to the length required.

Toile de Jouy lampshade

The inspiration for this embroidery came from a Toile de Jouy fabric that includes a romantic scene of a handsome young man courting a pretty maid. I decided to add the cheeky Cupid, ready to pierce the couple's hearts with his dart of love.

measurements

Worked on 16 count Aida, the finished embroidery measures 31 x 12.5cm (12¼ x 5in). Use 2 strands of cotton in the needle for cross stitch and 1 strand for backstitch and French knots. Work the French knots with 2 twists around the needle.

materials

To work the embroidery:
• Lampshade of your choice
• Tracing paper for pattern
• Piece of 16 count baby pink Aida, 5–7.5cm (2–3in) larger all round than lampshade pattern (see page 19)
• Stranded cotton embroidery threads as specified in the colour key
• Tapestry needle size 24 or 26
To make up the lampshade
• PVA adhesive or glue gun
• Cotton tape, 1.5cm (⅝in) wide
• Pink sewing thread
• Basic sewing kit
• Sewing machine

to make the pattern

Place the lampshade at one end of the piece of tracing paper and mark the position of the seam line. Roll the shade right round until the seam is back on the paper again, tracing the top and bottom outlines of the shade as you go. Add 1cm (⅜in) at each end and 2cm (¾in) at the top and bottom of the pattern shape, then cut out. Fold the pattern in half vertically, measure halfway down this fold line and mark in the central position for the embroidery on the pattern.

to work the embroidery

Cut out a piece of baby pink Aida to the appropriate size. As an example, the lampshade used here is 15cm (6in) deep; the bottom circumference is 78.5cm (31in) and the top circumference 28.5cm (11¼in). To allow enough room to fit in the pattern with 5–7.5cm (2–3in) all round, the Aida was cut to 61 x 35.5cm (24 x 14in).

Pin the pattern to the Aida and use a fabric marker to mark the outer edge of the pattern and the positions of the centre lines (1). Unpin the pattern and tack in the centre lines on the Aida to mark the centre position for the embroidery. Start stitching at the centre of the design and at the centre position marked on the Aida. To treat the finished embroidery, see page 104.

to make up the lampshade

Cut out the embroidered Aida into the lampshade shape and secure the raw edges with zigzag stitch. Wrap the fabric around the shade wrong side out, pinning the centre back seam to check the fit.

Remove the fabric from the shade, tack and machine stitch down the length of the seam and trim the seam allowance. Turn the embroidered lampshade cover through to the right side, press, and then put it back onto the shade. Apply glue to the top and bottom inside edges of the shade. Turn the top and bottom seam allowances to the inside, pressing them down onto the adhesive and snipping into the seam allowance to ensure a snug fit all the way around. Use clothes pegs to hold the fabric in place while the adhesive dries. When completely dry, glue on lengths of cotton tape to cover the raw edges of the fabric to give a neat finish.

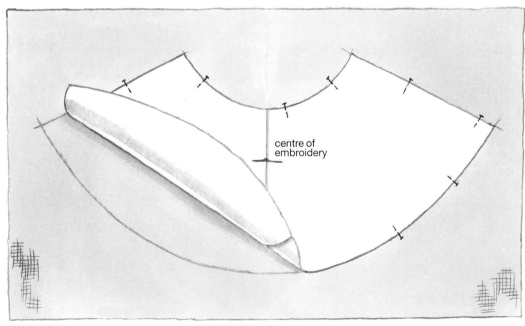

centre of embroidery

1

stranded cottons

DMC	Anchor	Skeins
3803	972	2
3685	1028	2
3350	78	2
3687	68	2
962	75	2
3326	25	2

French knots

DMC	Anchor	
154	72	1

Backstitch

DMC	Anchor
154	72

centre of design ▷

◁ centre of design

chapter 1 the living room

Folk art curtain tie

This embroidery was inspired by a carved wooden peacock from Sweden. The curtain tie can be stitched in white thread on red Aida, as here, or on a white background using red embroidery thread. The design is ideal to bring out for festive occasions.

measurements

Worked on 14 count Aida, the finished embroidery measures 34.5 x 6.5cm (13½ x 2½in). Use 2 strands of cotton in the needle throughout.

materials

To work the embroidery:

(for one curtain tie only)

• Tracing paper for template
• Piece of 14 count Christmas red Aida, 50 x 14cm (19¾ x 5½in)
• Stranded cotton embroidery threads as specified in the colour key
• Tapestry needle size 24 or 26

To make up the curtain tie:

• Piece of medium-weight interfacing, 50 x 14cm (19¾ x 5½in)
• Piece of red cotton fabric, 50 x 14cm (19¾ x 5½in)
• 23cm (9in) length of red cord
• Red sewing thread
• Basic sewing kit
• Sewing machine

to work the embroidery

Trace the curtain tie template on page 108, pin to the Aida and use a fabric marker to draw around the outline. Tack in the centre lines onto the Aida,

stranded cottons

DMC	Anchor	Skeins
321	9046	1
or		
blanc	2	1

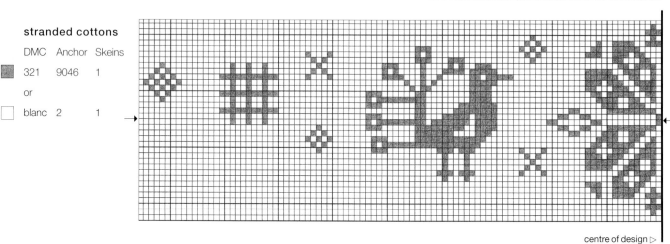

centre of design ▷

following the centre lines on the template. Do not cut out the curtain tie until the embroidery has been completed.

Start stitching at the centre of the design and in the centre of the Aida, following the chart. To treat the finished embroidery, see page 104.

to make up the curtain tie

Re-marking the outline if necessary, cut out the curtain tie shape, then use the template to cut out one piece in interfacing and one piece in red cotton backing fabric.

Pin and tack the interfacing to the wrong side of the embroidered Aida and zigzag stitch the two layers together. Place the cotton fabric and embroidered Aida right sides together and pin, tack and machine stitch the top (straight) edge of the curtain tie. Trim off the excess seam allowance and open out the cotton fabric away from the embroidered Aida and interfacing, then press the remaining seam allowance to the cotton side of the fabric. Topstitch the seam allowance down onto the right side of the cotton fabric as close to the edge as possible.

Fold the cotton fabric down onto the embroidered Aida, right sides together, and machine stitch the curved edges together, starting from one end, passing the middle, then leaving a gap of about 10cm (4in) slightly to one side of the middle of the curve and finishing the stitching at the other end.

Pull the tie to the right side through the open gap. Press to neaten the seam edges, at the same time pressing and turning in the open raw edges of the gap to the inside of the tie. Pin, tack and slipstitch the gap closed by hand, then press to neaten once again.

Push the raw end seam allowances to the inside of the tie. Cut the cord into 2 lengths of about 9cm (3½in), folding each piece in half to make a loop. Pin the 2 ends of one loop to the inside of one end of the curtain tie and backstitch the loop into position by hand, at the same time closing and securing the end of the curtain tie (1). (Handstitching is recommended because the fabric and loops together are too thick to pass through a domestic sewing machine.) Repeat for the other loop, at the other end of the curtain tie.

1

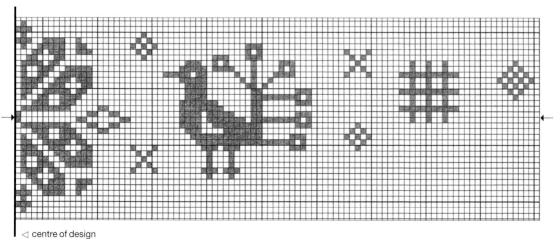

◁ centre of design

Wedgwood trinket box

The idea for this design came from a large dinner plate decorated with an idyllic country scene of meadows, farm animals, cottages and flowers. I took the flower motif from the border and adapted it to the circular shape of the trinket box lid.

measurements

Worked on 16 count Aida, the finished embroidery measures 13.3 x13.3cm (5¼x 5¼in). Use 2 strands of cotton in the needle for cross stitch and one strand for backstitch.

materials

To work the embroidery:

- Piece of 16 count antique white Aida, 25.5 x25.5cm (10 x 10in)
- Stranded cotton embroidery threads as specified in the colour key
- Tapestry needle size 24 or 26

To make up the trinket box:

- Unpainted circular lidded box, 46cm (18in) circumference x 7cm (2¾in) deep
- Burgundy, bright red and white acrylic paints
- 2.5cm (1in) firm-bristled paintbrush
- Double-sided adhesive tape, 1.5cm (⅝in) wide
- Piece of medium-weight cotton wadding, 18 x 18cm (7 x 7in)
- Clear adhesive
- Sheet of white A4 paper
- Basic sewing kit

to work the embroidery

Start stitching at the centre of the design and in the centre of the Aida, following the chart. To treat the finished embroidery, see page 104.

to make up the box

Add a blob of white and a smaller blob of bright red to burgundy acrylic paint until the colour matches DMC stranded cotton 3350/Anchor 42. Paint the body of the box inside and out. Set aside to dry.

Lay strips of double-sided adhesive tape on top of the box lid and peel off the backing. Lay the wadding on top of the lid and stick to the tape. Using scissors, trim away the excess wadding around the edge of the box lid.

Pin the finished embroidery to the top of the wadded box lid centring the design. Trim the excess Aida from around the embroidery, leaving enough fabric to be turned to the inside of the lid: you will need to allow for the depth of the lid rim plus about 2cm (¾in) to be glued to the inside of the lid.

Before gluing, place a strip of double-sided adhesive tape around the rim of the lid and press the tape over onto the underside of the lid. Peel off the backing and gently press the Aida onto the taped rim and towards the inside of the lid, carefully easing away the wrinkles as you go. Snip into the excess loose fabric on the underside of the lid, then place clear glue underneath the loose fabric and press down to flatten.

To neaten the underside of the lid and hide the raw edges of the Aida, cut a circle of white paper 0.3cm (⅛in) smaller all round than the lid. Glue the paper to the underside of the lid, cutting slits in the paper where necessary to allow the pieces of wood that secure the lid to the box to stick out.

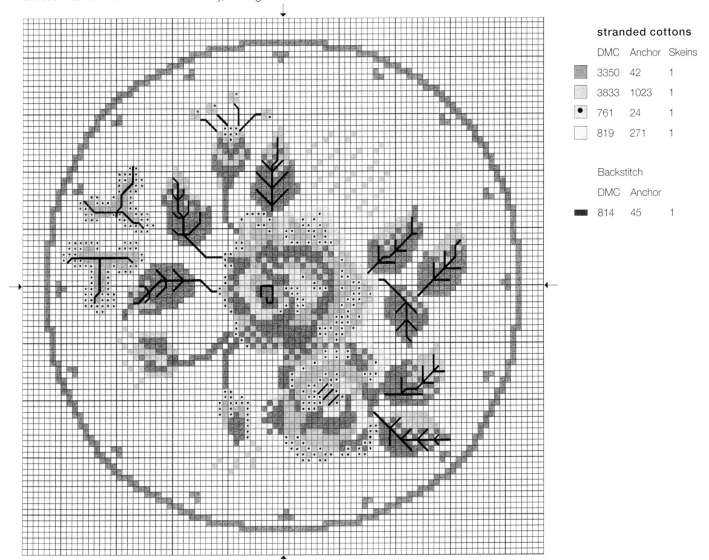

stranded cottons

	DMC	Anchor	Skeins
	3350	42	1
	3833	1023	1
●	761	24	1
	819	271	1

Backstitch

	DMC	Anchor	
	814	45	1

The kitchen

If you have a house full of people, the kitchen is the place where everyone usually congregates. It is the centre of the home, the place where we prepare the food to fuel our bodies and live healthily. The aroma of a delicious meal being cooked in the kitchen attracts everyone in the house, all ready to indulge in the fine fare.

Nowadays we have a huge choice of foods from all over the world, in a myriad of beautiful colours and shapes. There is a profusion of wonderful red shades: when shopping in the market, look at the bright reds of chillies, peppers and tomatoes, and the deeper shades of beetroot, red cabbage and aubergines. The fruit stalls look particularly inviting, decorated with plump, ripe red fruits – from rich pink raspberries and rhubarb, through bright red strawberries, cherries and redcurrants, to deep dark blackberries, plums and blackcurrants.

When unpacking your purchases, store all your spare bags in the embroidered holder with its cheery Portuguese cockerel design. Relax with a refreshing hot drink, placing the cups on pretty embroidered coasters, or eat a healthy salad accompanied by freshly baked bread, piled in a wicker basket lined with a Chinese design. I have provided a South American motif for napkins to protect your clothing from the crumbs, and a Greek design for a tea towel to use when the fun of eating is over. Your kitchen can be as international as the food you prepare in it.

Napkin ring and napkins

These three motifs are taken from a woven South American sash belt I bought many years ago. When you first look at the belt, the designs are not obvious, but on closer inspection you can see owls, a tropical bird of some kind and maize plants, intermingled with the woven pattern of the belt itself. I have used the owls as a motif for the napkin ring, while the maize and bird designs appear on the napkins. You could add these two to the corners of a tablecloth as well, or use them on square coasters. Try repeating the owl design horizontally on a coffee pot warmer or tea cosy, or to make a café curtain border.

measurements

Worked on 14 count Aida, the finished owl embroidery measures 14 x 5.5cm (5½ x 2¼in), the maize 6 x 8cm (2⅜ x 3¼in) and the bird 7 x 6.7cm (2¾ x 2⅝in). Use 2 strands of cotton in the needle throughout.

materials

To work the napkin ring embroidery:
• Tracing paper for templates
• Piece of 14 count cream Aida, 20 x 28cm (8 x 11in)
• Stranded cotton embroidery threads as specified in the colour key
• Tapestry needle size 24 or 26

To make up the napkin ring:
• Piece of stiff interfacing, 14 x 26cm (5½ x 10¼in)
• 52cm (20½in) length of natural cotton tape, 1.3cm (½in) wide
• Cream sewing thread
• Basic sewing kit
• Sewing machine

To work the napkin embroideries:
• 2 pieces of 14 count cream Aida, each 18 x 18cm (7 x 7in)
• Stranded cotton embroidery threads as specified in the colour key
• Tapestry needle size 24 or 26

To make up the napkins:
• 2 natural cotton napkins
• Cream sewing thread
• Basic sewing kit
• Sewing machine

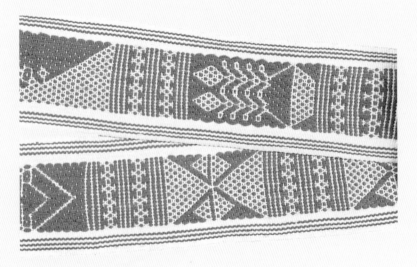

to work the owl embroidery

Trace the napkin ring template on page 107, pin to the Aida and draw around the outline with a fabric marker. Mark the centre of the embroidery position, then remove the template and tack the centre lines on the Aida. Do not cut out the napkin ring shape until the embroidery has been completed. Start stitching at the centre of the design and at the centre of the embroidery position on the Aida, following the chart. To treat the finished embroidery, see page 104.

to make up the napkin ring

Re-marking the outline if necessary, cut out the napkin ring shape and secure the raw edges of the Aida with zigzag stitch. With right sides together, pin, tack and machine stitch the long seam allowances together to make a tube.

Trace the interfacing template on page 107, pin the tracing paper pattern to the stiff interfacing and use a fabric marker to draw around the outline on the fold. Cut out the interfacing and machine stitch the 2 halves together along the 3 open sides, to achieve the correct thickness to slip into the napkin ring.

Turn the Aida tube right side out, placing the seam at the centre back of the embroidery. The sides of the napkin ring should follow the sides of the embroidery. Slip the interfacing inside the napkin ring. If the corners of the interfacing stick to the inside as you are trying to push it into the napkin ring, cut off about 0.3cm (⅛in) at each bottom corner of the interfacing. The interfacing should fit snugly inside the napkin ring. Turn in the 1cm (⅜in) seam allowance at each end of the napkin ring . Pin, tack and topstitch down each end, or slipstitch by hand.

Cut the length of cotton tape in half and fold the raw end of each half back on itself about 1.5cm (⅝in). Pin the folds (hiding the raw ends) to the back of each end of the napkin ring, tack and oversew by hand to secure (1). Slip the finished ring around a napkin.

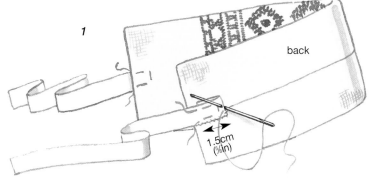

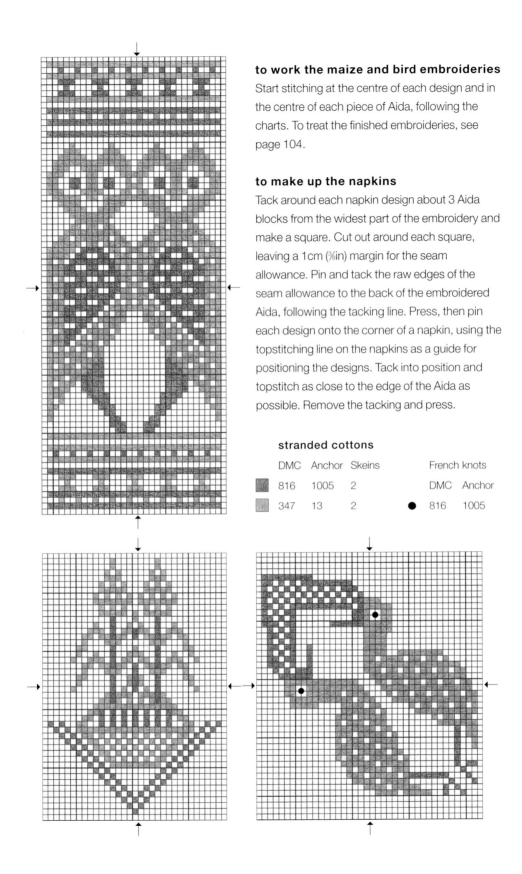

to work the maize and bird embroideries

Start stitching at the centre of each design and in the centre of each piece of Aida, following the charts. To treat the finished embroideries, see page 104.

to make up the napkins

Tack around each napkin design about 3 Aida blocks from the widest part of the embroidery and make a square. Cut out around each square, leaving a 1cm (⅜in) margin for the seam allowance. Pin and tack the raw edges of the seam allowance to the back of the embroidered Aida, following the tacking line. Press, then pin each design onto the corner of a napkin, using the topstitching line on the napkins as a guide for positioning the designs. Tack into position and topstitch as close to the edge of the Aida as possible. Remove the tacking and press.

stranded cottons

	DMC	Anchor	Skeins		French knots	
					DMC	Anchor
	816	1005	2			
	347	13	2	●	816	1005

Cockerel plastic bag holder

The idea for this design came from a cheerful reversible red and white tablecloth and napkins decorated with plenty of proud cockerels, which was sent to me as a gift by my family in Portugal. It can be stitched on red Aida using white embroidery thread, as here, but could also be worked on white Aida with red embroidery thread. Stuff the top of the holder with all the spare plastic bags you have and pull them out from the bottom as you need them.

measurements

Worked on 14 count Aida, the finished embroidery measures 15 x 16.5cm (6 x 6½in). Use 2 strands of cotton in the needle throughout.

materials

To work the embroidery:

- Piece of 14 count Christmas red Aida, 24 x 24cm (9½ x 9½in)
- Stranded cotton embroidery threads as specified in the colour key
- Tapestry needle size 24 or 26

To make up the holder:

- Piece of red cotton/linen mix fabric, 56 x 43cm (22 x 17in), plus extra 20 x 5cm (8 x 2in) for hanging loop
- Tracing paper for pattern
- 46cm (18in) length of elastic, 0.7cm (¼in) wide
- Red sewing thread
- Basic sewing kit
- Sewing machine

stranded cottons

DMC	Anchor	Skeins
321	9046	1
or		
blanc	2	1

to work the embroidery

Start stitching at the centre of the design and in the centre of the Aida, following the chart. To treat the finished embroidery, see page 104.

to make up the holder

BAG

Cut away excess Aida around the embroidery, leaving a 2cm (¾in) margin all round. Pin and tack the raw edges to the back of the fabric, leaving 3 Aida blocks visible around the outside edge of the embroidery.

Following the pattern diagram, make a tracing paper pattern and use it to cut out the bag shape from the cotton/linen fabric. Tack in the centre lines for the embroidery position and secure the raw edges with zigzag stitch. Pin and tack the embroidery into position and topstitch down onto the cotton/linen fabric, sewing close to the edge of the Aida. Machine stitch the side seam of the bag with a 1.5cm (⅝in) seam allowance.

TUNNELLING

Fold in the 2 raw ends of the bag by 0.7cm (¼in) and press. Fold in both ends again by 2cm (¾in) and press. Pin, tack and machine stitch along the very edge of each tunnelling fold, leaving a little gap. Cut the length of elastic in half, and thread a piece through the gap in each tunnelling fold using a bodkin or safety pin. Secure them by joining the ends with a few stitches sewn by hand. Both ends should now be gathered and elasticated.

HANGING LOOP

Cut a piece of the cotton/linen fabric 20 x 5cm (8 x 2in) and make a loop following the instructions on page 106. Fold the loop in half and hand stitch to the inside centre back of the top end of the bag.

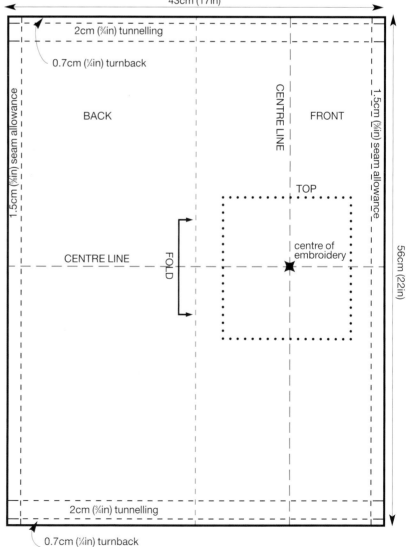

Chinese basket liner

A Chinese-style jar, decorated in terracotta reds, was the inspiration for this design. Line a wicker basket with the pretty embroidered cloth, fill with fresh crusty bread, and sit outside in the summer sun to enjoy a leisurely breakfast and let your cares just float away.

measurements

Worked on 14 count waste canvas, each finished small motif measures 9.5 x 5.5cm (3¾ x 2¼in) and the central motif 13 x 13cm (5⅛ x 5⅛in). Use 2 strands of cotton in the needle for cross stitch, backstitch on the antenna and French knots. Use one strand for backstitch on the temple. Work French knots with 2 twists around the needle.

materials

To work the embroidery:

- Circular wicker basket of your choice
- Tracing paper for pattern
- Length of string, drawing pin and cutting mat
- Piece of white cotton fabric, 9cm (3½in) larger all round than contoured measurement of basket (see below)
- Piece of 14 count waste canvas, 21.5 x 21.5cm (8½ x 8½in)
- Piece of medium-weight tear-away interfacing, 21.5 x 21.5cm (8½ x 8½in)
- 4 pieces of 14 count waste canvas, 10.5 x 17cm (4⅛ x 6⅝in)
- 4 pieces of medium-weight tear-away interfacing, 10.5 x 17cm (4⅛ x 6⅝in)
- Stranded cotton embroidery threads as specified in the colour key
- Tapestry needle size 24 or 26

To make up the basket liner:

- Piece of white cotton fabric, 9cm (3½in) larger all round than contoured measurement of basket (see below)
- Piece of medium-weight interfacing, 9cm (3½in) larger all round than contoured measurement of basket (see below)
- White cord, length of circumference of basket + 61cm (24in) for tying
- Adhesive tape
- 2 large wooden beads
- White acrylic paint
- White sewing thread
- Basic sewing kit
- Sewing machine

to make the pattern

Measure the inside of the basket, following the contour from rim to base to rim. As an example, the basket used here is 14cm (5½in) deep x 97.5cm (38⅜in) circumference and the contoured measurement is 46cm (18⅛in). Cut a piece of string half that measurement, in this case 23cm (9in), plus extra to tie around a drawing pin at one end and a pencil at the other.

Place the tracing paper on the cutting mat. Tie one end of the string to the drawing pin and stick it into the centre of the paper, then tie the other end around the pencil, making sure you keep the exact half measurement of the contoured diameter of the basket (in this case, 23cm/9in) between the drawing pin and pencil. Draw a circle with the pencil, keeping the string taut.

To draw the outer circle for the rim overlap, cord tunnelling and turnback, measure 6.5cm (2½in)

outwards from the first circle at several points and draw the circle following the measurements. The outer circle is the cutting line. The next line is the fold line for the 0.7cm (¼in) turnback for the raw edge. The next 2cm (¾in) is the fold line for the cord tunnelling and also the cutting line for the back of the liner and the interfacing. The last 4cm (1⅝in) is for the rim overlap.

Following the pattern diagram, mark in the embroidery positions on the tracing paper pattern, adjusting them as necessary according to the size of your basket.

to work the embroidery

Pin the tracing paper pattern to one piece of cotton fabric and cut out to the largest circle size. Tack in the centre lines on the straight grains of the fabric, also marking in the positions for the embroidery motifs.

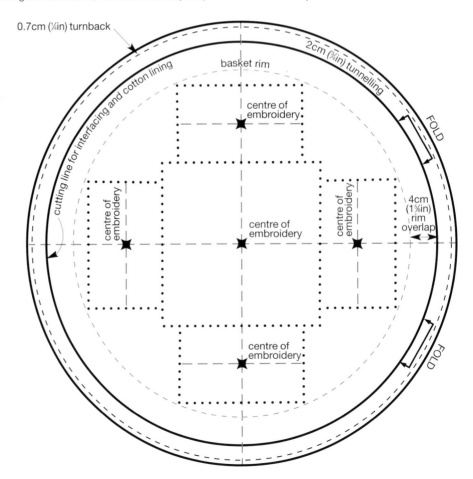

Prepare the waste canvas pieces and tack them into position, sandwiching the cotton fabric between the canvas and the tear-away interfacing (see page 100).

Start stitching at the centre of each motif and in the centre of each piece of waste canvas, following the charts. When the stitching is complete, remove the waste canvas and tear-away interfacing. To treat the finished embroidery, see page 104.

to make up the basket liner

Cut out one circle in cotton fabric and one in interfacing, following the fold line for the tunnelling. Pin them together and tack in the centre lines on the straight grain of the cotton fabric. Machine stitch the two layers together as close to the raw edges as possible.

Lay the interlined circle face down on top of the wrong side of the embroidered circle, matching the centre tacking lines. Pin and tack all 3 layers together, sewing on top of the line already stitched and as close to the raw edges as possible. Turn in the raw edges of the outermost circle to the back of liner by 0.7cm (¼in) and pin, tack and topstitch down. Press to flatten.

Turn in the 2cm (¾in) tunnelling for the cord to the back of the liner, using the stitching lines showing on the front as a guide and placing them towards the back of the liner with the tunnelling. Pin and tack the tunnelling down, then press to flatten the surplus fabric and make stitching easier. Machine stitch as close to the inside edge as possible, leaving a gap of about 1.5cm (⅝in) through which to thread the cord.

Cut the cord to length and stick a piece of adhesive tape to each end to prevent fraying. Thread the cord through the tunnelling using a safety pin (see page 106). Paint the wooden beads with white acrylic paint, allow to dry and then thread them onto the cord, knotting it at each end to prevent the beads slipping. Remove the tape and trim the ends of the cord to neaten.

stranded cottons

DMC	Anchor	Skeins
309	59	2
760	9	2
963	23	2

Backstitch

DMC	Anchor
3685	1028

French knots

DMC	Anchor	Skeins
3685	1028	1

Greek tea towel

In our family home we have a large collection of Greek ceramic coasters. In this modern design you can clearly see the near-Eastern influence.

measurements

Worked on 16 count Aida, the finished embroidery measures 5.5 x 29cm (2¼ x 11⅜in). Use 2 strands of cotton in the needle throughout.

materials

To work the embroidery:
- Piece of 16 count white Aida, 18cm (7in) deep x width of tea towel plus 3cm (1¼in)
- Stranded cotton embroidery threads as specified in the colour key
- Tapestry needle size 24 or 26

To make up the tea towel:
- Plain white waffle tea towel
- White sewing thread
- Basic sewing kit
- Sewing machine

to work the embroidery

Start stitching at the centre of the design and in the centre of the Aida, following the chart. To treat the finished embroidery, see page 104.

to make up the tea towel

Across the width of the Aida, there should be at least 10cm (4in) of unembroidered fabric at each end of the embroidery. For the depth, cut the Aida 3cm (1¼in) from the top and bottom of the embroidery, plus 1.5cm (⅝in) for each seam allowance. Secure the raw edges of the Aida with zigzag stitch. Tack along both long seam lines, following grain of the Aida, to achieve a good straight line. Turn, press and tack both long seam allowances to the wrong side of the Aida.

Pin the embroidered strip onto the tea towel about 6cm (2⅜in) up from the hem, folding in and pinning the side seam allowances to the wrong side of the Aida. Tack all round and topstitch down as close to the edge of the Aida as possible. Press the tea towel from the back to neaten the Aida strip.

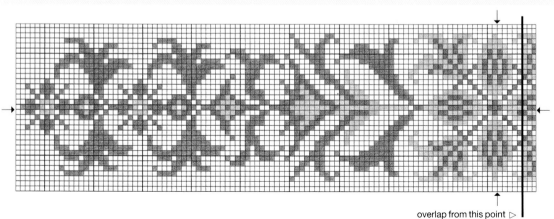

overlap from this point ▷

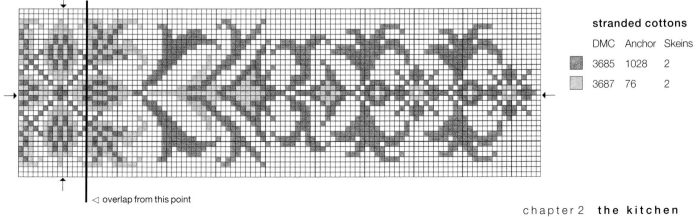

stranded cottons

	DMC	Anchor	Skeins
	3685	1028	2
	3687	76	2

◁ overlap from this point

William de Morgan coasters

The designs for these coasters were inspired by rich ruby-red lustre reproduction tiles in the style of the 19th-century ceramic artist William de Morgan. The sunflower and berry-and-leaf tiles have been adapted to make ideal designs for two coasters.

measurements

Worked on 16 count Aida, each finished embroidery measures 7.5 x 7.5cm (3 x 3in). Use 2 strands of cotton in the needle throughout.

materials

To work the embroidery:

- 2 pieces of 16 count cream Aida, each 23 x 23cm (9 x 9in)
- Stranded cotton embroidery threads as specified in the colour key
- Tapestry needle size 24 or 26

To make up the coasters:

- 2 pieces of thin wadding, each 9.5 x 9.5cm (3¾ x 3¾in)
- 2 pieces of plastic canvas, each 9.5 x 9.5cm (3¾ x 3¾in), or 2 acrylic coasters to take embroidery, each 8 x 8cm (3¼ x 3¼in)
- Cream sewing thread
- Basic sewing kit
- Sewing machine

to work the embroidery

Start stitching at the centre of each design and in the centre of the Aida, following the charts. To treat the finished embroideries, see page 104.

to make up each coaster

Lay the wadding on top of the plastic canvas. Join the 2 layers together by oversewing by hand, using the holes in the plastic canvas to secure. Tack in the centre lines on the wadded side and mark the centre back seam position on the plastic canvas with a fabric marker or pencil.

On the back of the embroidered Aida, mark the centre lines with tacking thread. Place the wadded canvas square, plastic side up, onto the back of the embroidery, matching the central tacking lines to centre the embroidery. To find the position of the centre back seam of the embroidered Aida, fold each side of the Aida

towards the middle of the plastic square, folding back the seam allowance at the marked centre line on the plastic canvas. Remove the wadded square and re-fold the Aida, wrong side out. Pin and tack the seam line at the point of the creased folds.

Still using the marked centre lines as a guide, place the wadded canvas square centrally on top of the tacked centre back seam line of the Aida and mark the position of the top and bottom seam lines on the Aida (1). Machine stitch down from each end of the centre back seam, to about 0.7cm (¼in) beyond the marked top and bottom seam lines (2). Leave a 1.5cm (⅝in) seam allowance and trim away the excess fabric.

Centre the back seam, then pin, tack and machine stitch the top and bottom seams at the marked positions. Trim the seam allowances to 0.7cm (¼in), cutting off the corners at an angle. Remove the tacking from the centre back seam. Turn to the right side and tease out the corners with a needle. Bend and push the wadded plastic canvas in through the open centre back seam, then oversew the seam closed by hand. Press lightly to neaten.

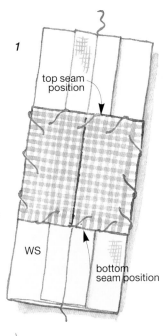

stranded cottons			stranded cottons		
DMC	Anchor	Skeins	DMC	Anchor	Skeins
902	45	1	349	1098	1
304	47	1			

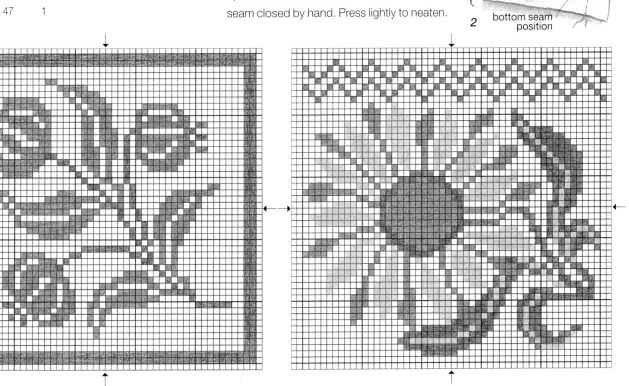

The bathroom

In past centuries bathing was a rare luxury, but today most of us are spoiled with an unending flow of hot and cold water, and are able to soak in a warm bubbly bath or enjoy a quick shower to relax and refresh us at any time we like.

The Ancient Romans understood the pleasures of truly luxurious bathing areas and they harnessed natural hot springs to create them. Our own bathrooms can provide a modern version with oversize

baths, jacuzzis and power-showers all widely available. For luxury to rival the Romans', add natural herb-scented soaps, aromatherapy bath oils, and beautiful hand-embroidered accessories.

Practicalities are catered for by a handy cosmetics bag embellished with a carnation motif, and wall-hung storage pockets to take all those small accessories that usually clutter up shelves and surfaces. Luxury items include a delightful chair back cover, pretty embroidered towels and soft, warm slippers sporting a pair of lazily buzzing bees. For a baby or young child, there is a cosy bath robe with a maritime theme – ideal to wrap around your freshly bathed little one while recounting adventure stories of pirates on the high seas.

Baby's bath robe

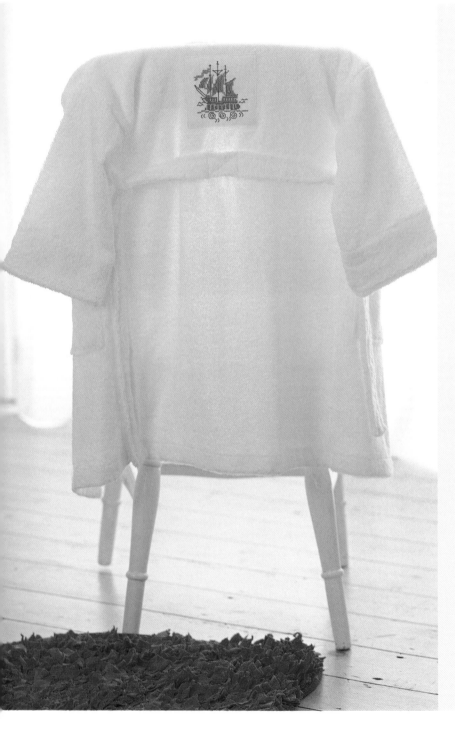

Embroider a pristine white baby's bath robe with a maritime motif appropriate to bathtime. This galleon in full sail was inspired by a tile that is a reproduction of one of William de Morgan's distinctive 19th-century red lustre designs. Here, the motif is placed on the back of the bath robe, but you could also use it on the pockets or at both corners of the front of the robe.

measurements
Worked on 14 count Aida, the finished design measures 8 x 9cm (3¼ x 3½in). Use 2 strands of cotton in the needle throughout, and work French knots with 2 twists around the needle.

materials
To work the embroidery:
• Piece of 14 count white Aida, 20 x 20cm (8 x 8in)
• Stranded cotton embroidery threads as specified in the colour key
• Tapestry needle size 24 or 26
To make up the bath robe:
• White towelling baby's bath robe
• White sewing thread
• Basic sewing kit
• Sewing machine

to work the embroidery

Start stitching at the centre of the design and in the centre of the Aida, following the chart. To treat the finished embroidery, see page 104.

to make up the bath robe

Measure the embroidered Aida into a 10 x 10cm (4 x 4in) square, centring the design, and add a 1cm (⅜in) seam allowance all round. Cut away excess Aida. Pin and tack the seam allowance to the back of the embroidery. Tack in the centre lines of the embroidery.

Fold the bath robe to find the centre back on the right side of the towelling and tack in its position. Place the bottom of the embroidered Aida about 4cm (1½in) up from the belt and insert a pin into the towelling as a marker. Measure up 5cm (2in) from the pin – this will be the position for the centre of the embroidery. Tack this horizontal centre line onto the robe.

Place the embroidery wrong side down on the right side of the towelling robe, in the marked position. Pin, tack and then topstitch the embroidery into place as close to the folded edge of the Aida as possible and press lightly from the inside of the robe.

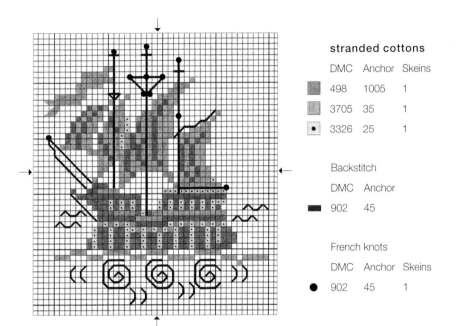

stranded cottons

DMC	Anchor	Skeins
498	1005	1
3705	35	1
3326	25	1

Backstitch

DMC	Anchor
902	45

French knots

DMC	Anchor	Skeins
902	45	1

Chair back cover

This chair back cover design came from a pretty porcelain Hungarian trinket box, given to my mother by her best friend. The box is lozenge shaped with a beautiful leaf and flower design on top and a delicate border of intertwined leaves and flowers.

measurements

Finished embroidery measures 24 x 8.2cm (9½ x 3¼in) on 14 count waste canvas. Use two strands of cotton in the needle for each cross stitch.

MATERIALS

To work the embroidery:
- 1 piece of cream fine linen fabric 61 x 84cm (24 x 33in) including 1.5cm (½in) for seam allowance
- 1 piece of 14 count waste canvas 35.5 x 18cm (14 x 7in)
- 1 piece of tear-away interfacing 35.5 x 18cm (14 x 7in)
- Stranded cotton embroidery threads as specified in the colour key
- Tapestry needle size 24 or 26

To make up the chair back cover:
- 1 piece of natural cotton lace 89cm (35in) long and about 3cm (1¼in) wide
- Cream sewing thread
- Basic sewing kit

to work the embroidery

Start by cutting out the linen to the measurements suggested above. Tack along the centre fold line of the fabric, so that the two longest edges are divided in half. On the left half of the fabric measure up 14 cm (5½ in) from the bottom raw edge, and tack in the horizontal line. Tack in the centre line of the embroidery position. Sandwich the centred linen between the waste canvas and the tear-away interfacing (see page 100). Start stitching at the centre of the design and in the centre of the waste canvas, following the chart. When the stitching is complete, remove the waste canvas and tear-away interfacing. To treat the finished embroidery, see page 104.

To make up the chair back cover

Cut the cotton lace into two pieces 44.5cm (17½in) long. You should have about 2cm (¾in) at each end for turning the raw edges in. Either oversew the turned-in raw edges of the lace by hand or topstitch down by machine. Place one piece of prepared lace, with the decorative edge facing towards the centre of the chair back, onto the raw edge of the linen, with one finished edge of the lace lying just inside the centre fold line of the linen. There should be 1.5 cm (½ in) left free for the seam allowance on the raw side seam of the linen. Repeat with the second piece of lace on the other side of the linen. Pin, tack and machine stitch the lace to the linen.

Fold the fabric in half, along the centre fold line, with right sides together. Pin, tack and sew all

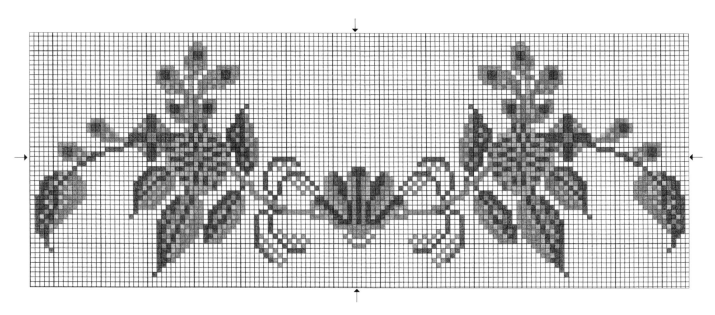

round the three raw edges making sure the lace
does not get caught in the sewing and is facing
inwards, towards the centre. Leave a 1.5 cm (½ in)
seam allowance all round. Leave an unsewn gap
of about 8–10 cm (3–4 in) along one of the edges
to pull the embroidery through to the right side.
Press to neaten on the back of the cover and
oversew the gap from the back of the work.

stranded cottons

DMC	Anchor	Skeins
815	1005	2
349	1098	2
760	1022	2

Bee slippers

Embroider a pair of waffle slippers with these charming little buzzing bees. The inspiration for the design came from a Toile de Jouy fabric with a beautiful exotic bird and flower pattern. The fabric also has the occasional insect flying in and out of the flora and fauna.

measurements

Worked on 14 count Aida, the finished embroidery (one bee) measures 4.3 x 4cm (1⅝ x 1½in). Use 2 strands of cotton in the needle throughout, and work French knots with 2 twists around the needle.

materials

To work the embroidery:
• 2 pieces of 14 count white Aida, 7cm (2¾in) larger all round than front of slippers
• Stranded cotton embroidery threads as specified in the colour key
• Tapestry needle size 24 or 26
To make up the slippers:
• Pair of white waffle slippers
• All-purpose adhesive
• White sewing thread
• Basic sewing kit
• Sewing machine

stranded cottons

DMC	Anchor	Skeins
3706	31	1
891	28	1
817	9046	1

Backstitch

DMC	Anchor
817	9046

French knots

DMC	Anchor	Skeins
817	9046	1

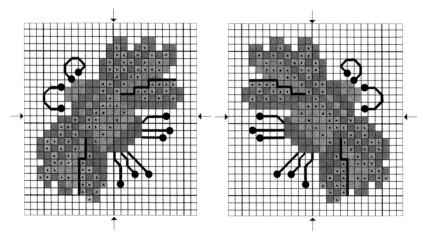

to work the embroidery

Start stitching at the centre of the design and in the centre of the Aida, following the chart. To treat the finished embroidery, see page 104.

to make up each slipper

Tack in the centre lines on the slippers and the embroidered Aida. Place the Aida over the front of one slipper and centre the design by matching the tacking lines. Pin the Aida to the front of the slipper, then pull out the tacking from the slipper, otherwise it will get stuck while you are stitching. Tack the Aida firmly onto the front of the slipper.

Trim away excess Aida, leaving a 3cm (1¼in) margin around the toe and 1.5cm (⅝in) around the top front of the slipper (1). Turn the 1.5cm (⅝in) raw Aida edge at the top of the slipper to the back of the embroidery, matching the Aida edge to the curved top shape of the top of the slipper. Tack the 2 layers together.

Using a large machine stitch, attach the Aida around the toe of the slipper by following the piping stitching line of the slipper underneath. Gather the seam allowance with a running stitch worked by hand close to the outer edge of the fabric and pull underneath, towards the sole of the slipper. Secure the gathering with a few stitches at the end of the line of running stitch.

Again using a large machine stitch, topstitch down the gathered seam allowance under the foot, by following the stitching line already sewn around the toe. Trim away excess Aida fabric

under the slipper 0.3–0.5cm (⅛–³⁄₁₆in) from the topstitching line and use a little all-purpose adhesive to glue the raw fabric edge to the sole of the slipper and prevent it from fraying.

Turn the slipper right side up and hand stitch the top curved edge of the Aida onto the slipper using a small backstitch or prick stitch. Remove all the tacking. Stuff the slipper with a piece of spare fabric to keep it in shape, then steam press the embroidery gently to neaten.

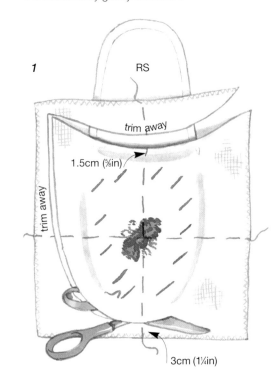

1   RS

trim away

1.5cm (⅝in)

trim away

3cm (1¼in)

Folk art hand towels

These two hand towels are decorated with simple motifs that use a single colour for each design, making them ideal for the less experienced cross stitcher or even complete beginner to work on as a first project. Both patterns were inspired by Polish folk art, which has its roots in the basic colours, plain fabrics and stylized motifs of flora and fauna that were available to the rural dwellers who originally developed these appealing naive designs.

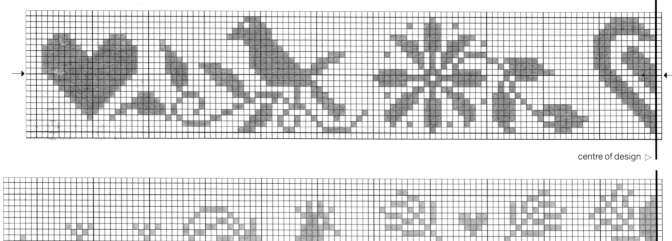

centre of design ▷

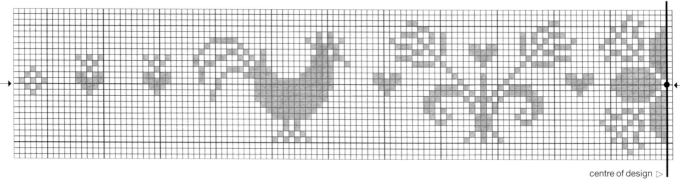

centre of design ▷

stranded cottons

DMC	Anchor	Skeins
150	59	2
3731	76	2

French knots

DMC	Anchor
● 3731	76

measurements

Worked on an Aida band (see below), the finished embroidery measures 38 x 3cm (15 x 1¼in) for the white towel and 40.5 x 4cm (16 x 1⅝in) for the pink towel. Use 2 strands of cotton in the needle throughout. Work the French knot on the pink towel with 2 twists around the needle.

materials

To work the embroideries:

• 2 white Aida bands, 5.5cm (2¼in) wide with 28 stitches across the width x 56cm (22in) long

• Stranded cotton embroidery threads as specified in the colour key

• Tapestry needle size 24 or 26

To make up the towels:

• 1 white and 1 dusty-pink hand towel, each 50cm (19¾in) wide

• White and dusty-pink sewing threads

• Basic sewing kit

• Sewing machine

to work the embroideries

Start stitching at the centre of each design and in the centre of the Aida, following the charts. To treat the finished embroideries, see page 104.

to make up each towel

Find the centre of the embroidered Aida band and of the width of the towel. Mark both centres with a pin. (Most towels have a flat woven strip across their width about 8cm (3¼in) up from both ends of the towel, and the pin marking the centre of the towel should be placed just next to it.)

With right sides up, place the centre of the embroidered Aida band on the centre of the towel over the flat woven strip. Pin, tack and topstitch the embroidered Aida onto the towel, leaving the raw edges free at each end.

Turn the ends of the Aida band to the back of the towel, folding over twice to hide the raw edges. Pin, tack and slipstitch to the towel.

◁ centre of design

◁ centre of design

chapter 3 **the bathroom**

Carnation cosmetics bag

The motif on this useful cosmetics bag is taken from one of my bargain finds, a pretty cake plate of unknown origin. The design is an unusual terracotta-coloured transfer print of ferns and carnations intertwined through circular hoops. If you find the prospect of making up the bag too daunting, transfer the design to the corners of a tablecloth, embroider curtain ties or even stitch it onto pockets to decorate a special item of clothing.

measurements

Worked on 16 count Aida, the finished embroidery measures 15.5 x 9cm (6⅛ x 3½in). Use 2 strands of cotton in the needle for cross stitch and one strand for backstitch.

materials

To work the embroidery:
• Tracing paper for template
• Piece of 16 count antique white Aida, 20 x 28cm (8 x 11in)
• Stranded cotton embroidery threads as specified in the colour key
• Tapestry needle size 24 or 26

To make up the cosmetics bag:
• Piece of ivory linen fabric, 51 x 51cm (20 x 20in)
• Piece of cotton lining fabric, 51 x 51cm (20 x 20in)
• Piece of medium-weight interfacing, 51 x 51cm (20 x 20in)
• 46cm (18in) length of red ribbon, 0.3cm (⅛in) wide
• Pearl or glass button, 1.5cm (⅝in) diameter
• Cream sewing thread
• Basic sewing kit
• Sewing machine

to work the embroidery

Following the pattern diagram, make a tracing paper pattern for the bag flap. Pin the flap pattern onto the Aida and either tack or draw around the outline with a fabric marker. Tack in the centre lines for the embroidery position. Start stitching at the centre of the design and the centre position of the embroidery, following the chart. To treat the finished embroidery, see page 104.

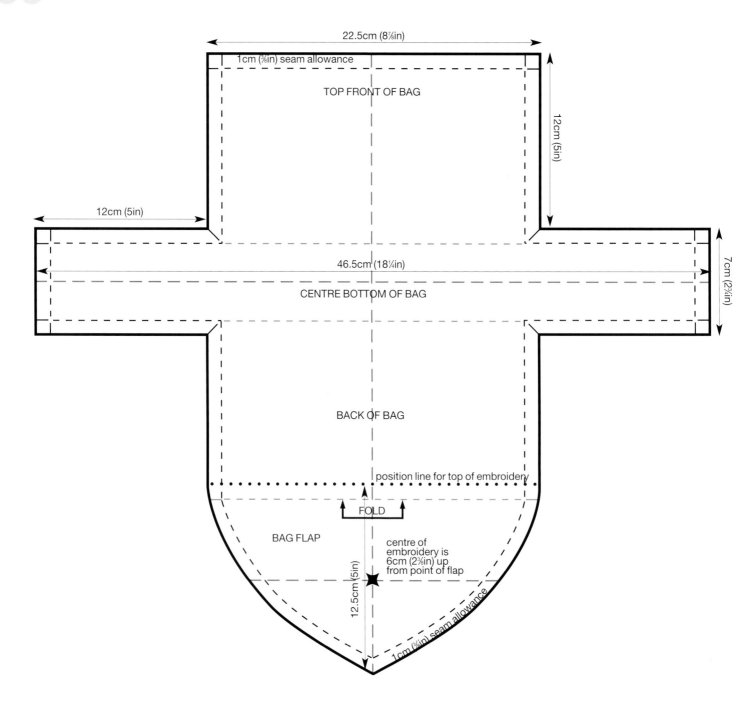

22.5cm (8⅞in)

1cm (⅜in) seam allowance

TOP FRONT OF BAG

12cm (5in)

12cm (5in)

46.5cm (18¼in)

7cm (2¾in)

CENTRE BOTTOM OF BAG

BACK OF BAG

position line for top of embroidery

FOLD

BAG FLAP

centre of
embroidery is
6cm (2⅜in) up
from point of flap

12.5cm (5in)

1cm (⅜in) seam allowance

to make up the bag

FLAP

Following the pattern diagram, make a tracing paper pattern for the main piece, then cut out one piece each from the linen fabric, lining and interfacing, and tack in the centre lines on all 3 pieces. Lay the interfacing on the wrong side of the linen and pin, tack and machine stitch the raw edges together with zigzag stitch.

Re-marking the outline if necessary, cut out the embroidered Aida to the flap pattern shape. At the top (straight) edge, turn back 1cm (⅜in) to the wrong side of the embroidery. Pin and tack the embroidered flap to the right side of the flap on the linen fabric, matching the centre lines. Topstitch the top edge of the Aida onto the linen, then machine stitch the remaining edges of the Aida to the linen with zigzag stitch.

stranded cottons

	DMC	Anchor	Skeins
■	221	20	1
■	817	13	1
■	351	10	1
•	3771	882	1

Backstitch

	DMC	Anchor
■	221	20

assembly

With wrong sides out, pin, tack and machine
stitch each of the 4 side seams of both the lining
and the embroidered linen (1). With right sides
together, pin and tack the lining and the
embroidered bag together, with the lining placed
inside the bag. Machine stitch together around
the edge, leaving a gap of about 6cm (2½in) on the
centre front of the bag (2). Trim excess seam
allowances, then pull the bag to the right side
through the gap and press to neaten. Pin and tack
around the flap and top edge of the bag opening,
closing the gap at the same time. Topstitch
around the flap first and then around the top edge
of the bag opening. Press to neaten.

finishing

Fold the length of ribbon in half and pin to the
inside of the flap 0.7cm (¼in) down from the flap
point. Secure by hand with a few stitches. Lay the
flap down onto the bag and sew the button onto
the linen to just below the flap point. Tie the ribbon
around the button to make a bow and cut the
ribbon ends to the length required.

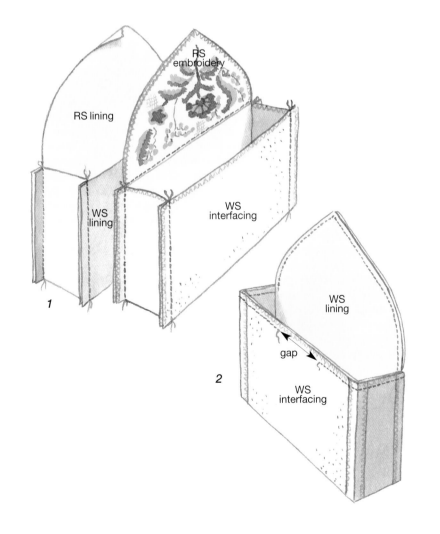

Hanging pockets

This design came from a calico fabric that is embroidered in rich red with a basket of flowers. The pockets are an ideal size for storing bathroom bits and pieces, and look good hung from a chunky wooden hook. You can adapt the idea as desired, making the fabric twice as long and adding two extra pockets at the bottom, or double the width by lengthening the dowelling and adding two more pockets on the sides. Repeat the embroidery on each pocket.

measurements

Worked on 14 count Aida, the finished embroidery measures 10 x 11½cm (4 x 4⅝in). Use 2 strands of cotton in the needle throughout.

materials

To work the embroidery:
- Tracing paper for pattern
- Piece of 14 count cream Aida, 36 x 28cm (14¼ x 11in)
- Stranded cotton embroidery threads as specified in the colour key
- Tapestry needle size 24 or 26

To make up the hanging pockets:
- Tracing paper for pattern
- Piece of cream linen fabric, 75.5 x 39cm (29¾ x 15⅜in), for main piece
- Piece of interfacing, 75.5 x 39cm (29¾ x 15⅜in)
- Piece of cream linen fabric, 32 x 22.5 (12⅝ x 8⅞in), for pocket lining
- Piece of medium-weight interfacing, 32 x 22.5 (12⅝ x 8⅞in)
- 37cm (14½in) length of wooden dowel, 1.5cm (⅝in) diameter
- 31cm (12¼in) length of natural cotton tape, 1.5cm (⅝in) wide
- Piece of cream linen fabric, 18 x 18cm (7 x 7in), for tassels
- 2 red beads with fairly large holes (see page 61)
- Cream sewing thread
- Basic sewing kit
- Sewing machine

▷

to work the embroidery

Following the pattern diagram, make a tracing paper pattern for the pockets. Pin the pattern to the Aida and mark out the pocket shape. Tack in the centre vertical dividing line for the pockets. On each pocket area, tack in the centre position for the embroidery. Start stitching at the centre of the design and in the centre of each pocket, following the chart. To treat the finished embroidery, see page 104.

to make up the hanging pockets

MAIN PIECE

Following the pattern diagram, make a tracing paper pattern for the main piece. Cut out one main piece from linen and one from interfacing. Lay the interfacing on the wrong side of the linen. Pin and tack the 2 layers together, then machine stitch the raw edges together with zigzag stitch. Fold the long sides in half, with the interfacing on the outside. Pin, tack and machine stitch down

the side seam and along the bottom. Pull through to the right side through the open top. Push out the bottom corners with a needle and press to neaten. Machine stitch the top edge closed with zigzag stitch.

stranded cottons

	DMC	Anchor	Skeins
■	815	1005	1
▨	347	19	1

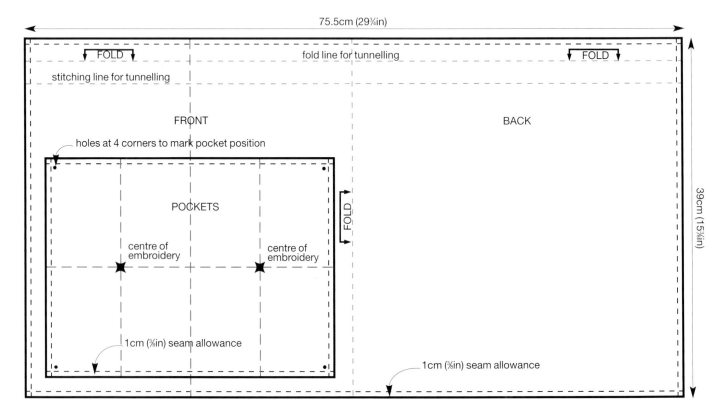

POCKETS

Cut out one pocket piece from linen and one from interfacing. Re-marking the outline if necessary, cut out the pocket shape from the embroidered Aida. Place the pocket interfacing on the wrong side of the linen pocket lining, then pin, tack and machine stitch the raw edges together with zigzag stitch. Place the lining and the embroidered Aida right sides together, then pin, tack and machine stitch the top seam of the pocket. Press the seam towards the lining side and topstitch down from the right side of the lining as close to the edge of the fabric as possible.

Fold the lining down onto the embroidered Aida, right sides together, then pin, tack and machine stitch down all 3 open sides, leaving a gap of about 8cm (3¼in) in the centre bottom. Trim the seam allowances and pull the pocket to the right side through the gap, pushing out the corners with a needle. Pin and tack the gap closed, and press to neaten.

On the main piece, pin and tack around the edge and down the centre of the pockets, about 3.5cm (1½in) from the bottom and sides of the main piece. Double topstitch down the centre first and then around the 3 sides of the pockets (1). Press to neaten.

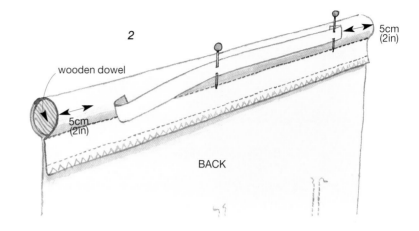

2

wooden dowel

5cm (2in)

5cm (2in)

BACK

TUNNELLING

At the top of the hanging, fold 4cm (1⅝in) to the back. From the folded top edge measure down 2.5cm (1in) and pin the fold together to make the tunnelling. Push the wooden dowel through the tunnelling to check that it fits correctly, adjusting the pins as necessary. Remove the dowel, then tack and machine stitch to make the tunnelling. Machine stitch another row of stitching to hold down the spare seam allowance at the back.

Fold in the 2 raw ends of the tape. Pin the tape to the centre back of the tunnelling and pin down the folded ends, keeping the tape taut and following the stitching line of the tunnelling. There should be a 5cm (2in) gap at each end. Oversew the ends of the tape securely to the tunnelling (2).

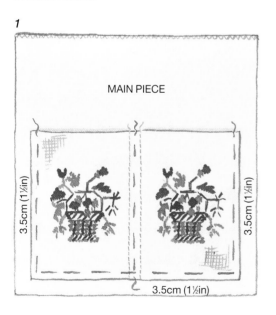

1

MAIN PIECE

3.5cm (1½in)

3.5cm (1½in)

3.5cm (1½in)

TASSELS

Cut 2 strips of linen fabric, each measuring 9 x 18cm (3½ x 7in). Fold the 2 long sides of each strip in half. Leaving a gap of 1.5cm (⅝in) from the folded top of each tassel, cut strips 0.7cm (¼ in) wide and 7.5cm (3in) long. Fold the raw side edges towards the middle, then roll the fabric round on itself to make a tassel. Neatly oversew the last roll to the tassel to secure. With cream thread, attach a bead to the top of each tassel with 3–4 sets of neat hand stitches. Stitch a beaded tassel to each bottom corner of the hanging (3). The snipped tassel ends are left raw.

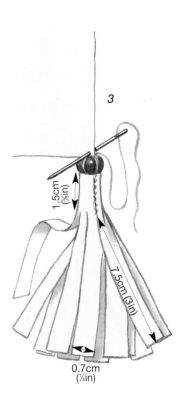

3

1.5cm (⅝in)

7.5cm (3in)

0.7cm (¼in)

The bedroom

The bedroom is a place of romance, peace and privacy, where you can rest and recuperate after a hard day's work. Relax and unwind in a calm room decorated in warm shades of red and white – cosy on a cold winter's night yet refreshing on a hot summer evening.

Pile the bed with comfortable, pretty cushions – this chapter includes a fleecy

rectangular cushion embroidered with an intricate Victorian tile motif, and a small circular velvet cushion with an unusual red and white Willow Pattern design. Crisply laundered sheets and pillowcases decorated with pretty embroidered roses will ensure a good night's sleep. To complete the effect, there is a dressing table mat and a wall-hung sampler, both with a Chinese theme.

I have also included a Toile de Jouy design for a baby's bedroom: a delightful cot quilt cover scattered with chubby cherubs, to ensure sweet dreams for the whole family.

Cherub cot quilt cover

I was delighted when I discovered this cheerful Toile de Jouy fabric design, featuring little cherubs flying among roses and playing chase with some fluttering (and somewhat startled) birds. I adapted the cherubs and birds for this pretty cot cover, as they seemed an ideal subject for a sleeping baby. Sweet dreams.

measurements

Worked on 14 count Aida, the finished embroidery measures 38.5 x 10cm (15¼ x 4in). Use 2 strands of cotton in the needle for cross stitch and French knots in the cherubs' hair. Use one strand for backstitch and French knots on the cherubs' navels and nipples, and on all eyes. Work all French knots with 2 twists around the needle.

materials

to work the embroidery:
- Piece of 14 count cream Aida, 3cm (1¼in) longer than width of quilt x 20cm (8in) deep
- Stranded cotton embroidery threads as specified in the colour key
- Tapestry needle size 24 or 26

To make up the quilt cover:
- Cot quilt
- Piece of pink cotton fabric to match DMC stranded cotton 3731/Anchor 38, wide enough to cut one side seam on the fold (see cutting diagram)
- Strip of medium-weight interfacing, same width as cotton fabric x 6cm (2⅜in) deep
- 5 buttons to match colour of cotton fabric or DMC stranded cotton 815/Anchor 1005, each 2cm (¾in) diameter
- Pink and cream sewing threads
- Basic sewing kit
- Sewing machine

to work the embroidery

Start stitching at the centre of the design and in the centre of the Aida, following the chart. To treat the finished embroidery, see page 104.   ▷

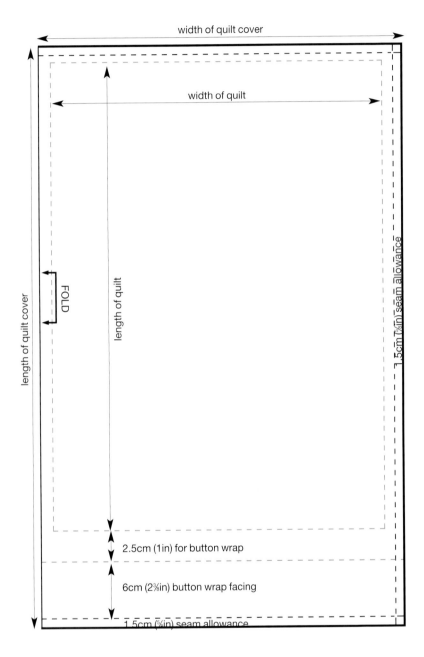

width of quilt cover

width of quilt

length of quilt cover

length of quilt

FOLD

1.5cm (⅝in) seam allowance

2.5cm (1in) for button wrap

6cm (2⅜in) button wrap facing

1.5cm (⅝in) seam allowance

to make up the cot quilt

ASSEMBLY

Following the cutting diagram, cut out the quilt cover from pink cotton fabric, marking in the seam and button wrap facing allowances. Tack in the vertical centre line for the front of the cover.

Prepare the embroidered Aida by trimming away excess fabric at the top and bottom, so that the band is 14cm (5½in) deep from raw edge to raw edge, and tack in the vertical centre line of the embroidery. Turn 1.5cm (⅝in) seam allowances at the top and bottom of the embroidered band to the wrong side and press, then repeat for the side seam that is on the side of the fold (the other end of the embroidered band will be sewn into the side seam of the cover).

Place the prepared embroidery right side up on the front of the quilt cover, across the width and 11.5cm (4½in) down from the top edge, and line up the tacking lines to centre the design. Pin, tack and topstitch the embroidered band to the quilt cover as close to the edge of the Aida as possible.

Pin, tack and machine stitch the interfacing onto the wrong side of the bottom of the quilt cover, stitching around the sides and bottom edge of the strip. Fold the quilt cover in half vertically, right sides together. Pin, tack and machine stitch the top and side seams. Leave the bottom of the quilt cover open. Trim away excess fabric from the seam allowances, cutting off the corners at an angle. Secure the raw edges with zigzag stitch. Turn the cover right side out and press. Turn the seam allowance at the open bottom edge of the cover to the inside and topstitch down.

BUTTONHOLES

Fold the button wrap facing to the inside of the quilt cover and to the edge of the interfacing. Press flat and tack down.

On the front of the cover, measure out 5 buttonholes evenly across the width, starting from the centre and 1.5cm (⅝in) up from the open end of the cover. Using pins as a guide, mark the

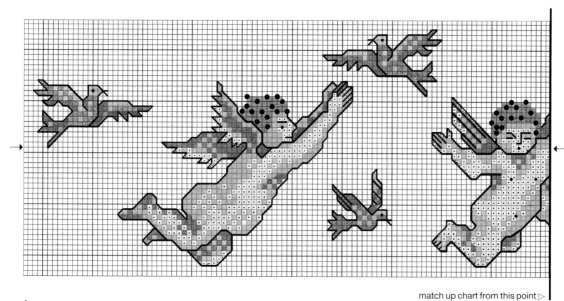

match up chart from this point ▷

◁ match up chart from this point

buttonholes with a fabric marker, 0.7cm (¼in) longer than the diameter of the buttons you are going to use. Make the buttonholes by machine or by hand, following the instructions on page 106.

Push a pin through the centre of each buttonhole to the fabric underneath and mark the position for each button on the inside back of the cover with a fabric marker. Stitch the buttons into position. Remove the tacking and press to neaten.

stranded cottons

	DMC	Anchor	Skeins
	902	45	1
	815	1005	1
	3731	38	1
•	605	1094	1

Backstitch			French knots		
DMC	Anchor		DMC	Anchor	
154	72		● 154	72 (eyes, navels, nipples)	
			● 902	45 (hair)	

Rose sheet and pillowcase

Crisp white sheets and pillowcases look lovely when embroidered with these attractive roses. The design came from an English red and white plate decorated with a repeat pattern of a cluster of roses. I used the rose in full bloom for the pillowcase design and the buds for the sheet edging.

measurements

Worked on 14 count waste canvas, the pillowcase motif measures 7 x 8cm (2¾ x 3¼in) and the sheet edging motif 20.5 x 3.7cm (8⅛ x 1⅜in). Use 2 strands of cotton in the needle throughout.

materials

To work the embroidery:
- White cotton sheet
- White cotton pillowcase
- 2 pieces of 14 count waste canvas, each 14 x 14cm (5½ x 5½in), for the pillowcase
- 2 pieces of tear-away interfacing, each 19 x 19cm (7½ x 7½in)
- Piece of 14 count waste canvas, 32 x 10cm (12⅝ x 4in), for the sheet edging
- Piece of tear-away interfacing, 32 x 10cm (12⅝ x 4in)
- Stranded cotton embroidery threads as specified in the colour key
- Tapestry needle size 24 or 26

To make up the sheet and pillowcase:
- Basic sewing kit

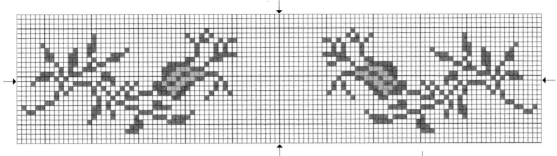

stranded cottons

	DMC	Anchor	Skeins
	3350	63	1
	3608	86	1
	153	95	1

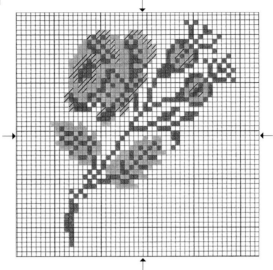

to work the pillowcase embroidery

To prepare the waste canvas, see page 100. In the top left-hand corner of the pillowcase, measure in 2cm (¾in) from each edge to find the position for the waste canvas. Avoiding the pillow flap inside, sandwich the pillowcase between the canvas and tear-away interfacing. Pin and tack into place, then find the centre position for the embroidery by measuring 7cm (2¾in) in from the canvas edges and tack in the centre lines (1). Repeat for the bottom right-hand corner by swivelling the pillowcase around so that the bottom right-hand corner is at top left.

Start stitching at the centre of the design and at the centre of the waste canvas, following the chart. Stitch into the top layer of the pillowcase only. When the stitching is complete, remove the waste canvas and tear-away interfacing. To treat the finished embroidery, see page 104. Press the pillowcase to neaten.

to work the sheet edging embroidery

To prepare the waste canvas, see page 100. Find the centre of the top edge of the sheet and tack in the centre vertical line for 16cm (6¼in) from the top edge. Tack in a horizontal line 8cm (3¼in) up from the top edge of the sheet. Find the centre of the waste canvas and mark it in (see page 101). Sandwich the sheet between the canvas and tear-away interfacing, matching the centre lines (see page 101) (2). Start stitching at the centre of the design and in the centre of the waste canvas, following the chart.

When the stitching is complete, remove the waste canvas and tear-away interfacing. To treat the finished embroidery, see page 104. Press the sheet edging to neaten.

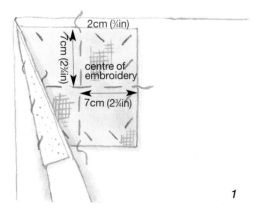

2cm (¾in)

7cm (2¾in)

7cm (2¾in)

centre of embroidery

1

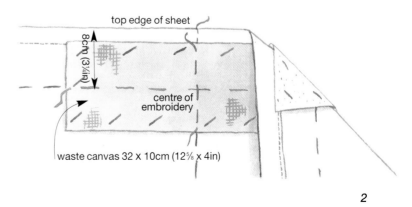

top edge of sheet

8cm (3¼in)

centre of embroidery

waste canvas 32 x 10cm (12⅝ x 4in)

2

Victorian tile cushion

A dear friend of mine lent me this tile which comes from an old Victorian house originally owned by her grandfather. The house faces the wild Atlantic coast and has panoramic views of the ever-changing colours of the sea and cliffs. The cushion is an ideal size to lean against comfortably and gaze out of the window, drinking in the beauty of the natural world.

measurements

Worked on 14 count Aida, the finished embroidery measures 18 x 38cm (7 x 15in). Use 2 strands of cotton in the needle throughout.

materials

To work the embroidery:
- Piece of 14 count antique white Aida, 23 x 43cm (9 x 17in)
- Stranded cotton embroidery threads as specified in the colour key
- Tapestry needle size 24 or 26

To make up the cushion:
- Feather cushion pad, 38 x 68cm (15 x 27in)
- Piece of red fleece fabric, 50 x 100cm (19¾ x 39⅜in)
- Piece of cream fleece fabric, 50 x 100cm (19¾ x 39⅜in)
- Red and cream sewing threads
- Basic sewing kit
- Sewing machine

to work the embroidery

Start stitching at the centre of the design and in the centre of the Aida, following the chart. To treat the finished embroidery, see page 104.

to make up the cushion

ASSEMBLY

If you cannot find a cushion pad of the required size, you can use an ordinary feather pillow. Narrow the pillow to 38cm (15in) by shaking down the feathers and folding the excess fabric to the inside of the pillow. Pin, tack and machine stitch down the long side of the pillow to make the size of cushion pad you want.

Cut the pieces of red and cream fleece to 41 x 71.5cm (16⅛ x 28⅛in) – the remainder of the fabric pieces will be used for making the tassels (see page 71). Tack in the centre lines on the cream fleece and the embroidered Aida.

Leave 2cm (¾in) on each long side of the embroidery and cut away the excess Aida fabric. Turn the long raw edges to the wrong side of the embroidery by 1cm (⅜in), leaving a gap from the embroidery to the folded finished edge of 1cm (⅜in). Pin, tack and topstitch the embroidery onto the fleece, as close to the edge of the Aida as possible, following the tacked centre lines to keep the design straight.

With right sides together, pin, tack and machine stitch the cream embroidered fleece front and red fleece back of the cushion cover together with a 1.5cm (⅝in) seam allowance, leaving a gap of 20–23cm (8–9in) at one of the short ends of the cover. Use red thread in the

sewing machine for the red fleece and cream thread for the cream fleece. Trim the corners of the cushion cover at an angle and trim away excess fabric from the seam allowances. Pull the cover to the right side through the gap and push out the corners with a needle. Stuff the cushion pad inside the cover and then oversew the gap by hand, making the stitches as invisible as possible. Fleece fabric does not need to be pressed.

TASSELS
From the spare pieces of fleece fabric, cut out 8 strips of red and 8 strips of cream, each 1.5 x 20cm (⅝ x 7⅞in), cutting in the direction of the selvedge to minimize the stretch. Place the strips

in the order cream, red, cream, red on top of each other, with 4 strips in each tassel. Stitch through the centre of each bundle by hand, winding the thread around the strips a few times each way and secure with a few stitches (1).
Stitch a tassel securely to each corner of the cushion by hand.

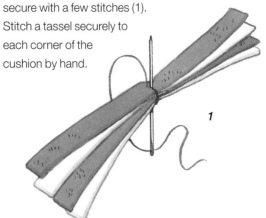

1

▷

stranded cottons

DMC	Anchor	Skeins
309	1025	3
816	1005	3

centre of design ▷

◁ centre of design

Willow Pattern cushion

Red and white Willow Pattern ceramics are not as popular as the blue and white version and are therefore not so easy to find. By chance, my neighbour is a great collector of mugs, jugs and plates – in fact, any ceramic artefact with a pretty design on it. She very kindly lent me a deep-pink Copeland china dish as a source for this cushion design. If making up the cushion is too daunting, you could have the embroidery professionallly framed in a circular picture frame.

measurements

Worked on 14 count Aida, the finished embroidery measures 18.5 x 17.5cm (7¼ x 6⅞in). Use 2 strands of cotton in the needle for cross stitch, French knots and backstitch on the tree above the house and the birds' beaks. Use one strand for all other backstitch. Work French knots with 2 twists around the needle.   ▷

materials

To work the embroidery:

- Piece of 14 count cream Aida, 35.5 x 35.5cm (14 x 14in)
- Stranded cotton embroidery threads as specified in the colour key
- Tapestry needle size 24 or 26

To make up the cushion:

- Tracing paper for pattern
- Piece of cotton lining fabric, 50 x 91cm (19¾ x 36in)
- Piece of wine-red cotton velvet, 1 x 1m (39⅜ x 39⅜in)
- Piece of medium-weight interfacing, 33 x 33cm (13 x 13in)

- Manmade fibre stuffing, enough to fill cushion pad (see page 71)
- Two 76cm (30in) lengths of piping cord
- 36cm (14¼in) length of cream or wine-red ribbon to match the velvet, 1cm (⅜in) wide (optional)
- Wine-red and cream sewing threads
- Basic sewing kit
- Sewing machine

to work the embroidery

Start stitching at the centre of the design and in the centre of the Aida, following the chart. To treat the finished embroidery, see page 104.

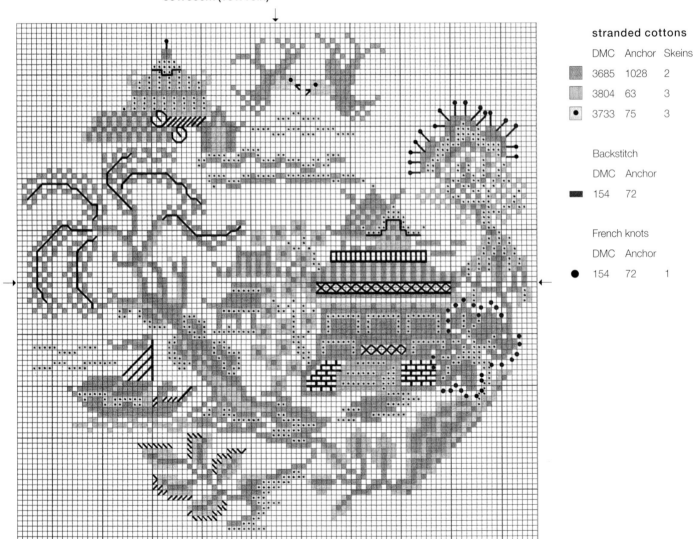

stranded cottons

	DMC	Anchor	Skeins
	3685	1028	2
	3804	63	3
	3733	75	3

Backstitch

	DMC	Anchor
	154	72

French knots

	DMC	Anchor	
●	154	72	1

to make up the cushion

CUTTING OUT

Draw a circle on tracing paper with diameter 24cm (9½in) and add 1cm (⅜in) all round for the seam allowance (see the method on page 36 for drawing a circle). Mark in the vertical and horizontal centre lines (diameters), cutting notches on the edge of the circle where the lines meet it to mark the balance points. Cut out 2 circles in cotton lining fabric, for the cushion pad. Cut out one circle in velvet and one in interfacing, for the cushion cover.

Draw a tracing paper pattern for the strip of fabric that goes around the circumference of the cushion, giving it its depth. Measure 79cm (31in) for the length of the strip and 7cm (2¾in) for the depth, which includes 1.5cm (⅝in) seam allowances all round. Notch in the seam allowances and the central balance marks on each side, matching these with the notches around the circumference of the circle. Cut one strip in cotton lining, for the cushion pad, and one strip in velvet, for the cushion cover.

CUSHION PAD

Fold the seam allowances at the short ends of the cotton lining strip to the wrong side and press. Pin, tack and machine stitch both cotton lining circles to the strip, matching the balance marks on the strip and circles. Where the two short ends of the strip meet, leave this open. Turn through to the right side, then pack in as much stuffing as possible to give the cushion pad a solid feel. Oversew the opening closed by hand.

CUSHION COVER

Place the interfacing circle onto the back of the embroidered Aida, matching the centre lines. Pin, tack and machine stitch around the edge of the interfacing with zigzag stitch, sewing it into position on the Aida. Cut away the excess Aida fabric to make the embroidered circle for the cushion cover.

1

PIPING

Cut 2 strips of velvet on the bias, each 79 x 4cm (31 x 1½in). Secure all the raw edges with zigzag stitch. Cover one length of piping cord with a strip of bias velvet and pin, tack and machine stitch down as close to the cord as possible. The velvet will extend beyond each end of the cord by 1.5cm (⅝in).

Pin and tack the covered piping onto the right side of the embroidered circle, with the raw edges of the piping to the raw edge of the circle and the raw ends sticking out from the edge of the circle and overlapping each other. The piping join is best placed at the bottom of the embroidered picture. Machine stitch the piping into position using a zipper foot, stitching as close to the edge as possible and over the overlapped piping ends to secure. Trim away the excess ends of the bias velvet (1). Repeat this procedure to cover the other length of piping cord and attach it to the velvet circle back of the cushion cover.

FINISHING

With the wrong side out, pin, tack and machine stitch the velvet strip ends to make a circle for the depth of the cushion cover. Pin, tack and machine stitch this circular strip to the embroidered cushion cover top with right sides together, using a zipper foot and stitching as close to the piping as possible. Repeat on the other side of the strip for the velvet cushion cover back, leaving a gap of 20–23cm (8–9in). Push the cushion pad inside the cover through the gap and oversew the gap closed by hand. If you like, make a ribbon bow to place at the bottom of the embroidered cushion to hide the piping join.

Dressing table mat

Three Chinese bowls, stacked with the smallest at the top and glazed on their undersides in a deep, rich pink with a filigree pattern of leaves, flowers and tendrils, were the inspiration for this embroidery. To ring the changes, you could embroider the leaf motif onto a duvet cover and pillowcases, cushion covers and other items, or stitch the full design on white Aida using red stranded cotton embroidery thread instead of the white on red here.

measurements

Worked on 14 count Aida, the finished embroidery measures 20.5 x 16cm (8⅛ x 6¼in). Use 2 strands of cotton in the needle throughout.

materials

To work the embroidery:
- Piece of 14 count Victorian red Aida, 53 x 24cm (20⅞ x 9½in)
- Stranded cotton embroidery threads as specified in the colour key
- Tapestry needle size 24 or 26

To make up the dressing table mat:
- Piece of white linen lining fabric, 59 x 30.5cm (23¼ x 12in)
- Cotton knit yarn, for tassels
- White sewing thread
- Basic sewing kit
- Sewing machine

to work the embroidery

Start stitching at the centre of the design and in the centre of the Aida, following the chart. To treat the finished embroidery, see page 104.

to make up the dressing table mat

Tack in the centre lines on the linen fabric, wrong side up. Tack in the centre lines on the embroidered Aida, right side up. Place the wrong side of the embroidery to the wrong side of the linen, with the right side of the embroidery uppermost. Match the centre tacking lines and pin and tack the 2 layers together, stitching around the edges of the Aida fabric.

Along both long raw edges of the linen fabric, turn a 1.5cm (⅝in) seam allowance towards the centre and press to flatten. Turn in once again by 1.5cm (⅝in), folding the linen over the edge of the Aida to act as a binding. Pin, press and tack the

binding onto the Aida. Repeat the process for the 2 short ends. Topstitch all round and as close to the bound edge as possible. Press to neaten and remove the tacking.

Make 4 tassels from the cotton knit yarn, following the instructions on page 17. Stitch a tassel to each corner of the mat by hand.

stranded cottons

DMC	Anchor	Skeins
321	9046	1
or		
blanc	2	2

overlap from this point ▷   ◁ overlap from this point

Chinese Toile sampler

Samplers were originally used as a stitch reference and an educational tool for young girls. The embroiderers recorded their family, places, flora and fauna in the stitched design, and usually signed and dated their work. These old samplers are now highly prized. The sampler I have designed was inspired by a fabric pattern called 'Chinese Toile'. I have not included an alphabet or numerals, but there is room at the top and bottom of the design to record your own details of the time, date and place at which the sampler was sewn, to be passed down to future generations.

measurements
Worked on 16 count Aida, the finished embroidery measures 21.5 x 14.5cm (8½ x 5¾in). Use 2 strands of cotton in the needle for cross stitch and one strand for backstitch and French knots. Work French knots with 2 twists around the needle.

materials
To work the embroidery:
• Piece of 16 count antique white Aida 38 x 27cm (15 x 10⅝in)
• Stranded cotton embroidery threads as specified in the colour key
• Tapestry needle size 24 or 26

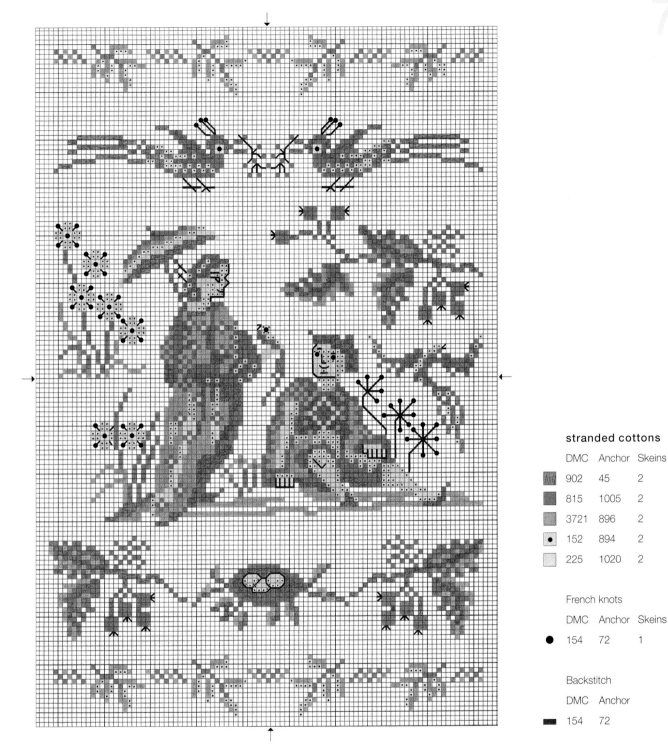

stranded cottons

	DMC	Anchor	Skeins
	902	45	2
	815	1005	2
	3721	896	2
●	152	894	2
	225	1020	2

French knots

	DMC	Anchor	Skeins
●	154	72	1

Backstitch

	DMC	Anchor
	154	72

To frame the sampler:
- Picture frame
- Acid-free mounting board
- Masking tape
- Strong thread and large needle

to work the embroidery

Start stitching at the centre of the design and in the centre of the Aida, following the chart. To treat the finished embroidery, see page 104.

to frame the sampler

Frame the sampler following the instructions given on page 106. Alternatively, you can take it to a professional framer.

Accessories and gifts

To present a gift to another person is an important gesture to show appreciation and thanks. We give gifts on many special occasions: the birth of a child, weddings, religious ceremonies, birthdays, anniversaries, yearly seasonal celebrations, and thanks for a good deed.

Give a special gift to a younger member of the family, to encourage them in their endeavours. The folk art-inspired pencil stand would make an ideal small token present for a hardworking teenager

studying for exams – fill the container with colourful pens or chocolates as an incentive to carry on the good work. For a budding young chef, a gift of the apron with its unusual dodo motif would inspire them to even more adventurous cooking.

Add to the romance of a wedding or St Valentine's Day by presenting a wall hanging of many hearts as a beautiful gift. A more practical present (perhaps for yourself), the Dutch Delft diary cover makes a perfect New Year gift. For those with equestrian interests there is a delightful horse picture, and the shoulder bag is a great gift for a close friend or relative whose tastes you know. It makes an unusual fashion accessory and would look wonderful against a natural linen suit or red velvet coat.

Folk art pencil stand

Original European folk art is difficult to find, but I have a wonderful book called *Folk Art of Europe* that was given to me by my father as a special gift. It illustrates a wealth of beautifully handcrafted designs in textiles, ceramics, wood and metal. The pencil stand embroideries here are adaptations from the hand-embroidered Danish designs of two vanity handkerchiefs stitched between 1818 and 1832.

measurements
Worked on 16 count Aida, each embroidery measures 8 x 8cm (3¼ x 3¼in). Use 2 strands of cotton in the needle throughout. Work French knots with 2 twists around the needle.

materials
To work the embroidery:
• Piece of 16 count antique white Aida, 30.5 x 18cm (12 x 7in)
• Triangular pencil stand
• Tracing paper for pattern
• Stranded cotton embroidery threads as specified in the colour key
• Tapestry needle 24 or 26
To make up the pencil stand:
• Piece of iron-on interfacing, 30.5 x 18cm (12 x 7in)
• Basic sewing kit
• Sewing machine

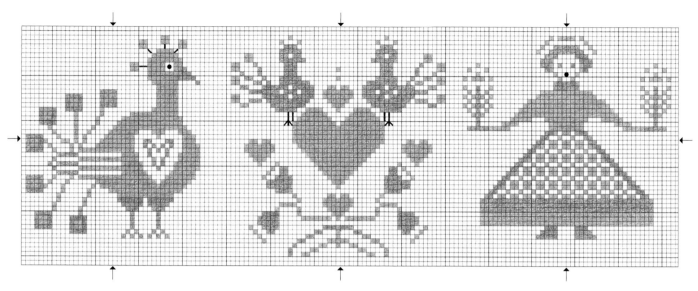

to work the embroidery

Tack in the centre lines on the Aida. Make a tracing paper pattern by drawing around the plastic liner inside the stand. Cut out the pattern and fold it in half lengthways, then unfold and mark in this centre line. Fold the pattern where the 3 facets of the plastic liner are divided, then unfold and mark in these dividing lines. Find the vertical centre line of each of the 3 facets by measuring and mark in their positions.

Place the pattern on the Aida fabric, keeping the horizontal and vertical centre lines in line with the horizontal and vertical grain of the Aida. Pin the pattern to the Aida and draw around the outline with a fabric marker, then mark the facet fold positions onto the fabric. Remove the pattern and tack in the horizontal centre line. Tack in the 3 vertical centre lines of the facets, to mark the centres of the embroidery positions (1).

Start stitching at the centre of each design and at each marked centre on the Aida, following the chart. To treat the finished embroidery, see page 104.

to make up the pencil stand

Iron the interfacing onto the back of the embroidered Aida to prevent the fabric from fraying. Re-marking the outline if necessary, cut out the fabric following the outline on the long sides and 3mm (⅛in) outside the outline on the short sides. Place the Aida inside the clear stand and insert the plastic liner to keep the embroidery in position.

stranded cottons

	DMC	Anchor	Skeins
	777	43	1
	347	19	2

Backstitch

	DMC	Anchor
	777	43

French knots

	DMC	Anchor
●	777	43

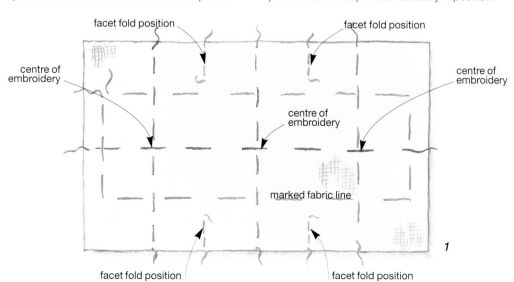

facet fold position

facet fold position

centre of embroidery

centre of embroidery

centre of embroidery

marked fabric line

facet fold position

facet fold position

1

Heart wall hanging

Toile de Jouy fabrics depict a myriad of beautiful birds, insects, plants, streams, lakes, classical buildings, people and mythical characters. Here I have picked out motifs from each of the toile fabrics used in this book and embroidered 6 hearts to make a wall hanging. Alternatively, work each design separately and frame them as a series of little pictures to hang on the wall or give as gifts, or embroider all 6 and hang them at different levels from a piece of bamboo to make an unusual mobile.

measurements

Worked on 14 count Aida, each finished embroidery measures 8 x 8cm (3¼ x 3¼in), except the bird with side borders which measures 8 x 12cm (3¼ x 4¾). Use 2 strands of cotton in the needle throughout. Work French knots with 2 twists around the needle.

materials
To work the embroidery:
- 6 pieces of 14 count cream Aida, each 16.5 x 16.5cm (6½ x 6½in)
- Stranded cotton embroidery threads as specified in the colour key
- Tapestry needle size 24 or 26
- 36 wine-red glass seed beads
- 14 white pearl seed beads
- Beading thread, to match Aida
- Embroidery beading needle

To make up the wall hanging:
- Tracing paper for template
- Piece of cream linen fabric, 37 x 50cm (14½ x 19¾in)
- Wadding, to stuff hearts
- 88cm (34¾in) length of cream satin ribbon, 0.7cm (¼in) wide
- Brass ring, 1.5cm (⅝in) diameter
- Cream sewing thread
- Basic sewing kit
- Sewing machine

to work the embroideries

Start stitching at the centre of each design and in the centre of the Aida, following the charts. Use the beading needle and beading thread when stitching on the beads (see page 104). To treat the finished embroideries, see page 104.

to make up the wall hanging

HEARTS

Trace off the heart template on page 108. Pin the template centrally over the embroidery, keeping the straight grain of the template on the straight ▷

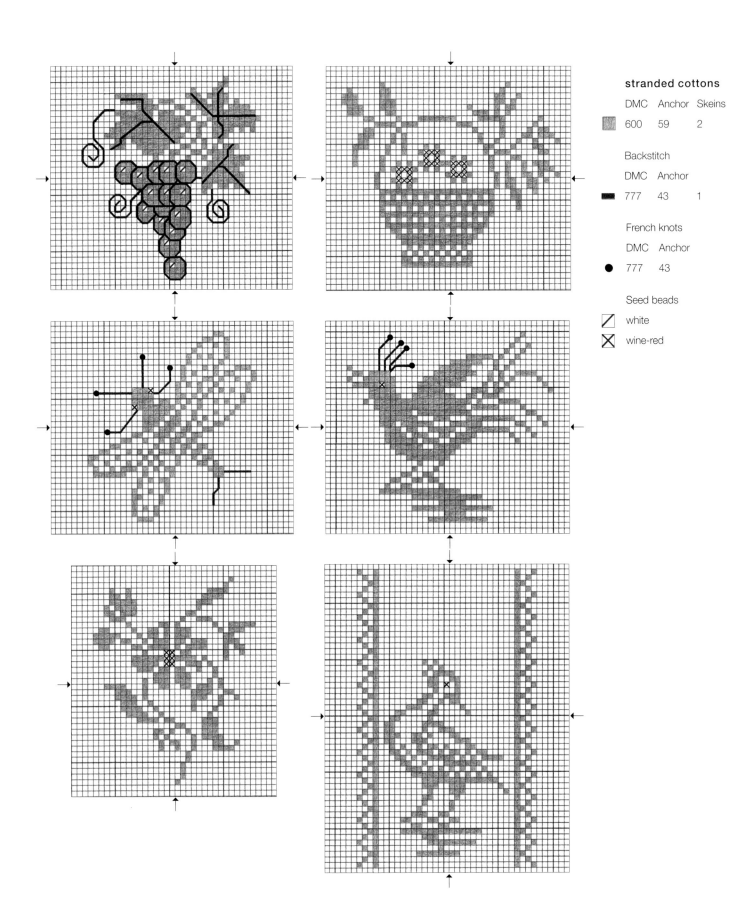

stranded cottons

DMC	Anchor	Skeins
600	59	2

Backstitch

DMC	Anchor	
777	43	1

French knots

DMC	Anchor
777	43

Seed beads

⟋ white

✕ wine-red

grain of the Aida fabric. Tack the heart shape onto the Aida around the outside edge of the template. Remove the template and repeat the process for each embroidered design.

Using a fabric marker and the template, trace out 6 heart shapes onto the linen fabric, keeping the straight grain of the template on the straight grain of the fabric. Mark a 1cm (⅜in) seam allowance around each heart, then cut out the linen hearts around the seam allowance line. Place the linen hearts onto the embroidered Aida, right sides together, matching the tacking line on the Aida with the drawn inner seam allowance line on the linen. Pin and tack the 2 layers together.

Start to stitch the hearts from one side, about 6cm (2⅜in) up from the bottom point, using a smallish stitch on the machine. Stitch around the heart and about 2cm (¾in) up past the bottom point. This will leave an open gap of about 4cm (1½in) (1). Trim off the excess seam allowance, leaving it intact across the gap. You may need to trim little V shapes at the topmost curved parts of the heart to get rid of excess fabric and snip to release the tension of the fabric at the top centre of the heart (see page 105). Secure the raw edges all round with zigzag stitch, leaving the edges across the gap unstitched. Pull through to the right side and press each heart.

Turn in and tack both sides of the raw edges across the gap, still leaving a hole. Stuff the heart with wadding, packing it in as neatly and tightly as possible. Stitch the gap closed by hand with very neat little oversewing.

ASSEMBLY

Loop the satin ribbon through the brass ring by 3cm (1¼in). Turn under the raw end of the ribbon by 0.5cm (¼in) and oversew by hand to secure the ring to the ribbon.

Pin the length of the ribbon at the centre back of each heart, making a row of hearts one above the other with gaps of 2cm (¾in) between them, placing the ring at the top heart. Oversew the

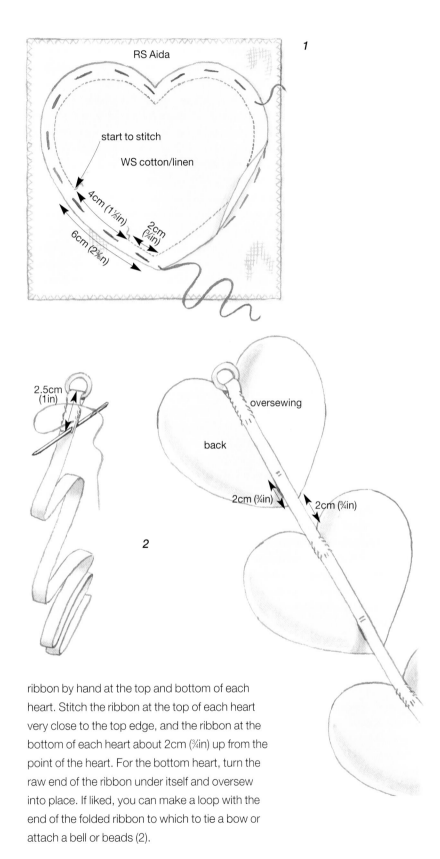

ribbon by hand at the top and bottom of each heart. Stitch the ribbon at the top of each heart very close to the top edge, and the ribbon at the bottom of each heart about 2cm (¾in) up from the point of the heart. For the bottom heart, turn the raw end of the ribbon under itself and oversew into place. If liked, you can make a loop with the end of the folded ribbon to which to tie a bow or attach a bell or beads (2).

Horse picture

The idea for this picture came from a Wedgwood teacup and saucer. The teacup has delicate roses on it, and the saucer has a rose border to match the cup framing a charming country scene. The horses grazing in a typical rural setting make the framed picture an ideal gift for a friend or relative with equestrian interests. Alternatively, you could stitch the finished embroidery onto a small cushion.

measurements

Worked on 14 count Aida, the finished embroidery measures 15 x 13cm (6 x 5⅛in). Use 2 strands of cotton in the needle for cross stitch and one strand for backstitch.

materials

To work the embroidery:
• Piece of 14 count antique white Aida, 32 x 32cm (12⅝ x 12⅝in)
• Stranded cotton embroidery threads as specified in the colour key
• Tapestry needle 24 or 26
To frame the sampler:
• Picture frame
• Acid-free mounting board
• Masking tape
• Strong thread and large needle

to work the embroidery

Start stitching at the centre of the design and in the centre of the Aida, following the chart. To treat the finished embroidery, see page 104.

to frame the picture

Frame the picture following the instructions given on page 106. Alternatively, you can take it to a professional framer.

stranded cottons

	DMC	Anchor	Skeins
■	915	102	1
✕	150	59	1
▨	3687	76	1
▢	3354	74	1
●	963	23	1

Backstitch

	DMC	Anchor	
▬	154	72	1

Dutch Delft diary cover

Dutch Delft ceramic ware is generally known for its handpainted blue and white designs. The Dutch ceramic beer mug from which I adapted this design commemorates 100 years of a particular make of lager and, unusually, is handpainted in red and white in the Delft style. The centre of the mug design consists of the traditional picturesque windmill, surrounded by a border of flamboyant flowers from which I have adapted the design for the diary cover. The Delft motif could be adapted to any diary of a similar size.

measurements

Worked on 16 count Aida, the finished embroidery measures 21.3 x 18.5cm (8⅜ x 7¼in). Use 2 strands of cotton in the needle throughout.

materials

To work the embroidery:
• Piece of 16 count antique white Aida, 23 x 27cm (9 x 10⅞in)
• Stranded cotton embroidery threads as specified in the colour key
• Tapestry needle size 24 or 26

To make up the diary cover:
• Tracing paper for pattern
• Piece of ivory linen fabric, 61 x 49cm (24 x 19¼in)

- Piece of medium-weight interfacing, 46.5 x 27cm (18¼ x 10⅞in)
- 56cm (22in) length of wine-red ribbon, 0.7cm (¼in) wide
- Piece of white touch-and-close fastening, 3 x 2.5cm (1¼ x 1in)
- A5 day-per-page diary
- Cream sewing thread
- Basic sewing kit
- Sewing machine

to work the embroidery

The Aida fabric will cover the front and the spine of the diary, with an overlap beyond the spine of about 3cm (1¼in). With the Aida placed with the short sides at top and bottom, count in 62 blocks from the right-hand long side and tack in a vertical line at this point, then tack in the centre horizontal line. The intersection marks the centre position for the embroidery.

Start stitching at the centre of the design and at the centre on the Aida, following the chart. To treat the finished embroidery, see page 104.

to make up the diary cover

ASSEMBLY

Following the pattern diagram, make a tracing paper pattern and use it to cut out 2 pieces from linen and one piece from interfacing. Lay the interfacing on the wrong side of one of the linen pieces and machine stitch the 2 layers together with zigzag stitch.

Tack down the vertical centre of the spine position and the horizontal centre line on the embroidered Aida. Turn the 2 vertical raw edges of the Aida to the back of the embroidery by 1cm (⅜in), pin and tack down.

Cut the length of ribbon in half and pin, tack and machine stitch one half onto the centre front of the linen/interfacing diary cover, just before the

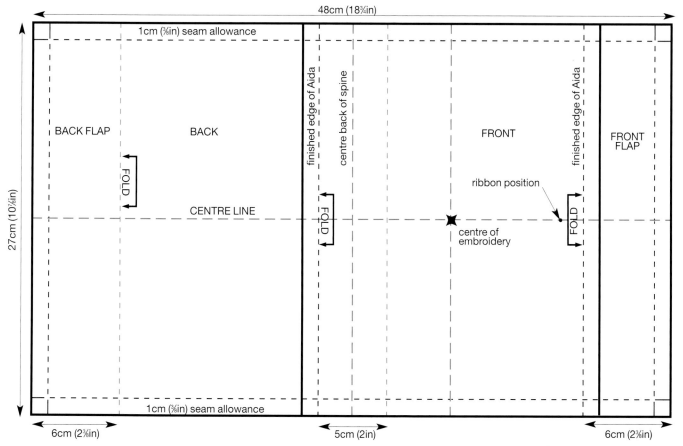

stranded cottons

DMC	Anchor	Skeins
814	70	2
3803	69	2
3731	76	2
761	1021	2

fold line of the diary edge as shown on the pattern (1). Place the prepared embroidery right side up onto the right side of the linen diary cover, matching the centre tacking lines. Pin, tack and topstitch down the 2 side edges of the embroidered Aida (2).

Place the linen lining onto the embroidered diary cover, right sides together, and pin, tack and machine stitch around all 4 edges, leaving a gap of about 8cm (3¼in) at the back flap of the cover. Make sure you push the front ribbon to the inside, so that it does not get caught while you are stitching. Pull the cover through to the right side and press to neaten.

POCKET FLAPS

Place about 1.5cm (⅝in) of the end of the other half of the ribbon to the inside centre of the open gap. Pin, tack and machine stitch into position, then turn the ribbon to the outside of the back flap and topstitch down to just before the diary edge. Fold the back flap at the fold line of the diary edge, towards the inside of the embroidered diary cover. Pin, tack and topstitch as close to the top and bottom folded edges as possible, to make the pocket flap for the back of the diary.

Cut the touch-and-close fastening in half lengthways. To make a pocket for the front of the diary, separate the touch-and-close and place the corresponding pieces opposite each other on the inside of the front flap and inside of the front of the embroidered diary cover. Position and machine stitch the outer pieces at the top and the bottom corners of the flap, as close to the edges of the flap as possible. Hand stitch the corresponding pieces into position on the inside of the front cover, so that no stitches show from the right side and when the flap is folded to the inside of the diary cover the matching pieces of touch-and-close lie exactly on top of each other (3).

FINISHING

Place the diary inside the cover, tie the ribbon and cut to the length required. Cut the ends of the ribbon at an angle.

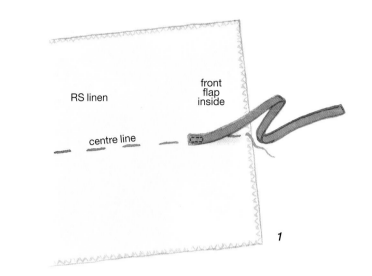

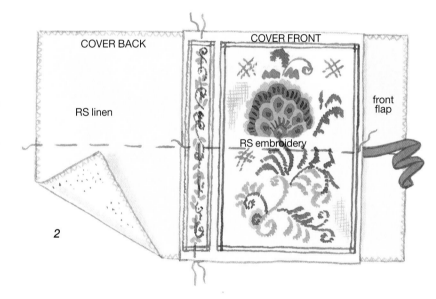

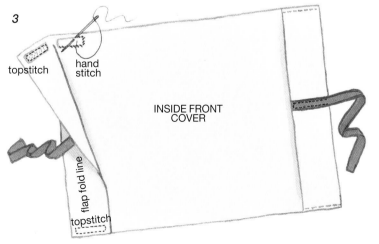

93

chapter 5 **accessories and gifts**

Tile shoulder bag

This design is taken from another tile lent to me by the same friend who lent me the Victorian tile on page 70. This tile is of a later date than the Victorian design used for the cushion cover, possibly from the art nouveau period which ran from the end of the 19th century to World War I. I have adapted the design to embroider the flap of an unusually shaped shoulder bag.

measurements
Worked on 14 count waste canvas, the finished embroidery measures 16 x 14cm (6¼ x 5½in). Use 2 strands of cotton in the needle throughout.

materials
To work the embroidery:
• Tracing paper for template
• Piece of cream cotton/linen mix fabric, 64 x 51cm (25 x 20in)
• Piece of 14 count waste canvas, 28 x 28cm (11 x 11in)
• Piece of tear-away interfacing, 28 x 28cm (11 x 11in)
• Stranded cotton embroidery threads as specified in the colour key
• Tapestry needle size 24 or 26
To make up the bag:
• Piece of cotton lining fabric, 64 x 51cm (25 x 20in)
• Piece of medium-weight interfacing, 64 x 51cm (25 x 20in)

• 1.83m (72in) length of wine-red twisted cord to match DMC stranded cotton 814/Anchor 45
• Shell pearl button, 2.5cm (1in) diameter, or button of your choice
• Small packet of wine-red glass seed beads
• Adhesive tape
• 2 wooden beads, each 6cm (2⅜in) circumference x 2.5cm (1in) long, with holes large enough to take twisted cord
• Cream sewing thread
• Basic sewing kit
• Sewing machine

To work the embroidery
Following the pattern diagram, make a tracing paper pattern. Secure the raw edges of the cotton/linen mix fabric with zigzag stitch. Lay the tracing paper pattern onto the right side of the cotton/linen fabric, with the straight grain of the pattern to the straight grain of the fabric. Pin the pattern to the fabric and draw around it with a fabric marker. Remove the pattern from the cotton/linen fabric and tack in the centre lines for the embroidery design.

Prepare the waste canvas and tack it into position, sandwiching the cotton/linen fabric between the canvas and the tear-away interfacing (see page 100).

Start stitching at the centre of the design and in the centre of the waste canvas, following the chart. When the stitching is complete, carefully remove the waste canvas and tear-away interfacing. To treat the finished embroidery, see page 104.

▷

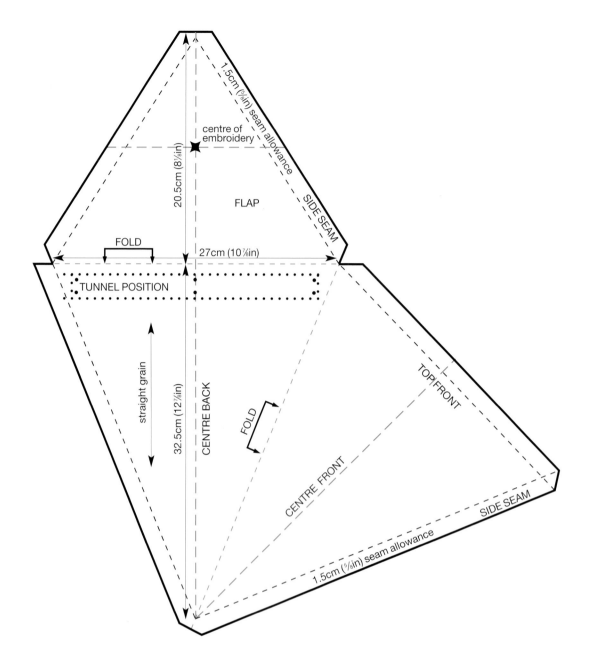

1.5cm (⅝in) seam allowance

centre of embroidery

20.5cm (8⅛in)

FLAP

SIDE SEAM

FOLD

27cm (10⅝in)

TUNNEL POSITION

straight grain

32.5cm (12⅞in)

CENTRE BACK

FOLD

CENTRE FRONT

TOP FRONT

SIDE SEAM

1.5cm (⅝in) seam allowance

to make up the bag

CUTTING OUT

Cut out one pattern piece from cotton lining fabric and one piece from interfacing. Re-marking the outline if necessary, cut out the embroidered cotton/linen fabric to the pattern shape. Lay the interfacing onto the wrong side of the embroidered fabric, then pin, tack and machine stitch the 2 layers together around the bag shape with zigzag stitch.

TUNNELLING AND BUTTON LOOP

Cut a strip of cotton/linen mix fabric for the cord tunnelling 6 x 25cm (2⅜ x 9⅞in). With right sides together, fold the strip in half lengthways. Pin, tack

and machine stitch the 2 long edges together with a 1cm (⅜in) seam allowance.

Placing the seam in the middle of the tunnelling, press and machine stitch one end of the tunnelling down flat with a 1cm (⅜in) seam allowance. Trim the seam allowances and carefully pull the tunnelling through to the right side. Press to neaten. Push the raw edge of the open end of the tunnelling to the inside of the tunnelling by 1cm (⅜in), press, then tack and topstitch the open end closed.

Pin the tunnelling onto the marked position on the right side of the back of the bag. Machine stitch along the 2 long edges of the tunnelling, leaving the 2 ends open.

Cut an 8cm (3¼in) length of cord and fold it in half to make a loop for the button. Attach the loop to the embroidered point of the bag, with the loop facing in towards the top edge of the bag. Tack and machine or hand stitch into position.

ASSEMBLY

Lay the lining onto the embroidered side of the bag with right sides together. Pin, tack and machine stitch around the flap and the front top edge of the bag opening, leaving the side seams unstitched. Trim the seam allowances, machine stitch around the sewn raw edges with zigzag stitch and pull through to the right side. Press the sewn seam to neaten.

Pin the lining side seams to the bag side seams, then tack and machine stitch each side

seam. With right sides together, pin, tack and machine stitch the side seams together to make the bag pouch. On the side seams, trim the top corner, bottom point and the seam allowance to neaten, then secure the raw edges with zigzag stitch. Pull through to the right side and press to neaten, pressing the button loop gently so that it will remain facing towards the bottom of the bag.

FINISHING

To find the position for the button, push in a pin just behind the bottom of the button loop and mark this point. Stitch the button into position. Make a tassel with stranded cotton embroidery thread DMC 814/Anchor 45 following the instructions on page 17. Hand stitch the tassel to the bottom point of the bag.

Thread some of the beads onto stranded cotton embroidery thread DMC 814/Anchor 45 and wind round where the bottom point of the bag and the tassel meet, securing with a few stitches. Repeat for the waist of the tassel.

Stick a piece of adhesive tape around each end of the remaining twisted cord. Using a safety pin, pass the cord through the tunnelling (see page 61). Push the ends of the cord through the wooden beads and knot the ends to secure. Tie the cord ends together to make the shoulder strap, adjusting the length as needed. Fray each knotted end to finish.

stranded cottons

	DMC	Anchor	Skeins
	814	45	2
	3722	1027	2
●	3354	25	1

Dodo apron

This dodo motif was inspired by one of William de Morgan's delightful animals. He designed many imaginary, mythical and real creatures, painting them onto his ceramics. Embroider the motif onto a pocket, placing it in any position you like on the apron. The ruby-red lustre colours will brighten up a kitchen, making cooking much more fun.

measurements

Worked on 14 count Aida, the finished embroidery measures 13.5 x 14cm (5⅜ x 5½in). Use 2 strands in the needle throughout. Work French knots with 2 twists around the needle.

materials

To work the embroidery:
- Piece of 14 count cream Aida, 29 x 25cm (11⅜ x 10in)
- Stranded cotton embroidery thread as specified in the colour key
- Tapestry needle size 24 or 26

To make up the apron:
- Tracing paper for template
- Cream-coloured apron
- Piece of cotton lining fabric, 17.5 x 18.5cm (6⅞ x 7¼in)
- Piece of medium-weight interfacing, 17.5 x 18.5cm (6⅞ x 7¼in)
- Cream sewing thread
- Basic sewing kit
- Sewing machine

to work the embroidery

Start stitching at the centre of the design and in the centre of the Aida, following the chart. To treat the finished embroidery, see page 104.

to make up the apron

Draw a rectangle measuring 17.5 x 18.5cm (6⅞ x 7¼in) onto tracing paper and mark in a 1cm (⅜in) seam allowance all round. Tack in the centre lines for the embroidery position on the apron and the centre lines on the embroidered Aida. Place the template over the embroidery, centring the design, and cut the embroidered Aida to size.

Place the cotton lining fabric right side up on top of the interfacing and secure the edges together with zigzag stitch. Place the embroidered Aida onto the interfacing, right sides together. Pin, tack and machine stitch the top seam of the pocket and trim away the excess seam

allowance. Open out the interfacing away from the embroidery, then press and topstitch the seam towards the interfacing side of the pocket from the right side of the interfacing, as close to the edge as possible.

Place the facing and embroidery right sides together again, keeping the topstitched seam towards the inside of the pocket (interfacing side) so that it will not show from the outside. Pin, tack and machine stitch the 2 side seams. Machine stitch the bottom edge of the pocket, leaving a 6cm (2⅜in) gap in the centre. Trim the seam allowances and snip off the corners of the pocket at an angle. Pull the pocket to the right side through the gap and push out the corners with a needle. Pin and tack the gap closed and press. Slipstitch the gap closed by hand.

Press the pocket and pin onto the tacked position on the apron. Tack and then topstitch the pocket into position. Press to neaten.

stranded cottons

	DMC	Anchor	Skeins
▨	815	1005	1
▨	321	9046	2
●	3712	10	1

Backstitch

	DMC	Anchor	Skeins
▬	3354	74	1

French knots

	DMC	Anchor
●	815	1005

Materials and techniques

This chapter provides all the information you need to work the embroideries in this book and make them up into stylish gifts or items for your home. The techniques are all very straightforward, and by following the instructions carefully you will be able to achieve results to be proud of every time.

MATERIALS AND EQUIPMENT
fabrics for cross stitch

The majority of the projects in this book are stitched on a blockweave fabric called Aida, while some of the items use waste canvas.

AIDA

To make a perfect square with each cross stitch, you need to use an evenweave fabric. This means that over a given length the fabric has the same number of threads woven into it vertically (warp) as horizontally (weft), so that the cross stitches – and therefore the designs – will not be distorted.

Aida is the easiest fabric on which to work cross stitch embroidery. The weave forms distinct blocks (hence 'blockweave') with relatively large holes in between, making it easy to count and to stitch.

Aida fabric is available in various colours and 'counts'. The count is the number of blocks of threads per 2.5cm (1in): Aida ranges from 8 to 18 count. The higher the count, the larger the number of stitches per 2.5cm (1in) and the smaller an embroidery with a given number of stitches will be.

WASTE CANVAS

Using waste canvas allows you to embroider directly onto most fabrics, even if the weave is not even or it is not possible to count the threads. Aida waste canvas is used for the projects in this book and ranges from 8 to 14 count. Tacking this gridded canvas on top of the fabric makes it possible to work the design easily, and the use of tear-away interfacing underneath the fabric stabilizes the embroidery.

To use waste canvas, position the canvas on top of the fabric that you wish to embroider and place the tear-away interfacing underneath, to make a sandwich. Tack securely, then embroider the design through all three layers. When you have finished, trim the waste canvas carefully around the completed embroidery, leaving a margin of

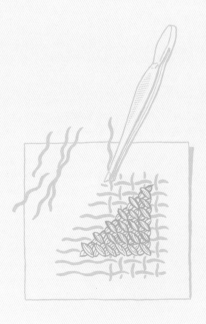

embroidery needles

Tapestry needles have large eyes for ease of threading and blunt points that will not separate and split the fabric threads. A size 24 or 26 needle is suitable for all the projects in this book.

embroidery threads

Several different types of thread are suitable for working cross stitch. However, all the projects in this book were stitched using stranded embroidery cottons. These fine cottons are supplied in a small skein and consist of six strands of thread, loosely twisted together. This enables you to cut off the length of thread you require (no more than about 45cm (18in), otherwise it may tangle while you are stitching), and to use varying numbers of strands in the needle – separate the individual strands and recombine the number required to ensure a good finish to the stitching. The number of strands required is specified for each project; as a general guide, for cross stitch on 14 to 16 count Aida you should use two strands, while on 18 to 20 count you should use one. You can vary the texture of your embroidery by experimenting with different numbers.

STITCHING THE DESIGN
preparing the fabric

Cut the fabric to the size required and secure the raw edges by oversewing with zigzag stitch on your sewing machine or alternatively by binding with masking tape.

For each project, the position of the embroidery will vary according to the design of the object, but in every case the method for centring the cross stitch design on the Aida fabric is the same. Always leave plenty of spare fabric around the embroidery, particularly with small items that might not otherwise fit an embroidery hoop (see page 102).

CENTRING ON AIDA

To centre the design on Aida, fold the fabric in half both ways, making visible crease lines; the point at which these lines intersect marks the centre of the design. Tack in the two crease lines in a contrasting thread. Match the centre of the chart (see Reading the charts, page 102) to the centre of the marked fabric and start stitching at this point. If the design is not to be placed centrally, then work out the approximate area in which it will be placed from the project instructions, then mark and tack in the vertical and horizontal centre lines of this area.

CENTRING ON WASTE CANVAS

Tack in the centre lines on the fabric you are using, in the same way as on Aida. Since you cannot fold the waste canvas, refer to the project instructions for the dimensions of the finished design and use these as a guide. Your stitching area on the canvas must be greater than these dimensions, and you must allow a margin for fixing the hoop (see page 102). Establish a boundary for the design, then mark in the centre lines with a fabric marker or tacking stitches. They will cross at the centre point of the canvas. Repeat to mark the centre point of the interfacing. Use the tacking lines to line up the centre points on waste canvas, fabric and interfacing. Secure all three layers in a 'sandwich' with firm tacking before starting to stitch.

EMBROIDERY HOOPS

Although it is possible to work your design while simply holding the fabric in your hand, it is far more satisfactory to use a hoop to keep the work taut and the stitches neat. An embroidery hoop consists of two rings, one smaller than the other. To fix the fabric into the hoop, stretch it over the smaller ring and then place the larger ring over the top, tightening the integral screw to keep the fabric in position. To protect the fabric from being marked by the hard edge of the smaller ring over which it is stretched, it is best to bind the ring with strips of fabric first. Hoops are available in a range of sizes from 10cm (4in) to 30cm (12in) in diameter.

reading the charts

Each project in this book is accompanied by a chart on which each coloured square represents one cross stitch. Backstitch is shown by a black (or coloured) line and French knots by a filled black circle. Beads are shown as a black cross or diagonal line. Where there are blank squares in the design, the fabric should be left unstitched.

Where squares are shown divided diagonally, with half the square in one colour and half in another (or left blank), three-quarter and quarter cross stitches are needed. When a divided square is on the edge of the design, work a three-quarter cross stitch to fill in the coloured area shown on the chart. When a square within the design is divided, stitch one part as a three-quarter cross stitch and the other part as a quarter cross stitch.

The colours of the chart squares correspond to those in the accompanying colour key, with the numbers alongside indicating the colour codes for the appropriate threads in both DMC and Anchor systems. The designs in this book were stitched with DMC stranded embroidery cottons. The nearest equivalent Anchor thread number has been provided for each, but if you use Anchor threads your finished work may not match the photographed embroideries exactly.

Before starting to stitch, refer to the chart for the project and check the dimensions of the design given alongside. Find the centre point of the design with the aid of the arrows marked on the sides of the chart. From the vertical arrow, trace a straight line downwards through the chart to the bottom; from the horizontal arrow, trace another straight line across the chart to the other side. The intersection is the centre of the design.

Start stitching at the centre of the design and keep a careful count of the stitches as you work, following the design accurately. It is best to work each small area of one colour and then change the thread to the next colour to work the adjacent stitches. In this way, you are likely to make fewer mistakes in counting than if you work all the stitches of one colour before changing thread. You may like to use a ruler or a piece of card to mark off each area of the chart as you complete it; this will help you to concentrate on one area at a time.

stitch techniques

CROSS STITCH

To start working in cross stitch, do not tie the thread in a knot, since this will show as an unsightly bump on the finished embroidery and may eventually come undone and loosen the stitches in the design. Instead, secure the thread by sewing one or two backstitches (see page 103) in an area that will eventually be covered up with cross stitches. Alternatively, leave a tail of thread and hold it in position at the back of the fabric so it will be caught in the cross stitches as you sew.

stranded cottons

DMC	Anchor	Skeins
814	45	2
304	47	3
350	11	1

French knots

DMC	Anchor
● 154	72

Backstitch

DMC	Anchor
▬ 154	72

Sample chart and colour key

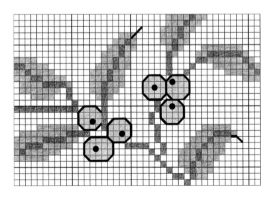

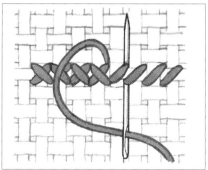

Cross stitch

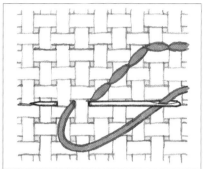

Backstitch

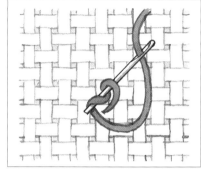

French knot

If you are working in a small area and diagonally, it is better to complete each cross stitch before moving on to the next. To work a single cross stitch, bring the needle up through to the front of the fabric at the bottom left of the stitch and take it back down through at the top right. Bring it up again at the top left and take it back down at the bottom right.

If you are working in a large area and horizontally or vertically, work from right to left and from top right to bottom left to make a row of diagonal stitches. When you have worked the correct number of stitches, work back along the row, crossing the diagonal stitches from top left to bottom right.

Whichever way you work, the top stitches of all the crosses must lie in the same direction, otherwise the work will appear uneven.

To secure a new thread and to finish stitching, slide the needle under several stitches already worked and cut off the thread neatly.

BACKSTITCH

This stitch is used for outlining or highlighting. Starting with the needle at the back of the fabric, bring it through to the right side of the fabric and make a backward stitch, passing the needle to the back of the fabric. Bring the needle up through to the right side of the fabric again, the length of one stitch ahead of the previous stitch. Continue in this way, following the chart for the direction of the stitches, remembering that the understitch is always twice as long as the top stitch.

FRENCH KNOTS

These are round, raised bobbles that are useful for representing eyes, the centres of flowers and so on. Bring the needle up through to the right side of the fabric in the position of the French knot. Twist the thread around the needle once, twice or three times, depending on the size of knot required. Holding the thread firmly with your thumb, push the needle down through the fabric in a position very close to where it first emerged. Hold down the knot with your thumb. Pull the thread to the wrong side of the fabric and secure the knot with one or two small stitches.

QUARTER AND THREE-QUARTER CROSS STITCH

To work a quarter cross stitch, bring the needle up through to the front of the Aida at the top left and take it back down again in the centre of the Aida square. To work a three-quarter cross stitch, bring the needle up through to the front of the fabric at the top right and back down again at the bottom left, over the quarter cross stitch.

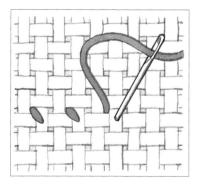

Quarter cross stitch

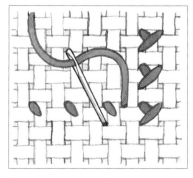

Three-quarter cross stitch

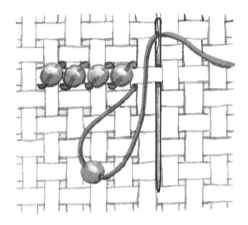

BEADING

To incorporate beads into a cross stitch
embroidery, you will need to use beading thread
and an embroidery beading needle. Match the
thread colour to that of the Aida, so that you can
use the same colour thread with any colour bead.
To start to stitch, secure the thread at the back of
the Aida with a few small backstitches and push
the needle up through to the front of the fabric at
bottom left. Thread the bead onto the embroidery
beading needle and take the needle back down
through the fabric at top right – the bead replaces
the embroidered cross. Work a line of beading in
this way, from left to right, with the beads all lying
in the same direction. If you have to leave a gap in
the beading, this should be no more than four
beads as otherwise you will lose the tension of the
beading. For a larger gap, or to finish beading,
secure the beads with a few small backstitches at
the back of the fabric.

When pressing your finished embroidery (see
below), take care to use the iron very gently as
otherwise you may distort the beads.

washing and pressing

When you have completed the design and
removed all the waste canvas and interfacing, if
used, wash the finished embroidery in warm water
with a gentle soap powder to remove any dirt that
has got onto it during the stitching. To remove
moisture, roll up the embroidery in a towel, then

place it face down on a towel and press on the
wrong side of the fabric with an iron on a low
setting to flatten the finished embroidery. Allow the
work to dry thoroughly before mounting it as a
picture or making it up into the finished item.

MAKING UP
basic sewing kit

To make up the projects in this book, you will need
the following basic sewing kit. For most, a sewing
machine is also required.

- paper scissors
- fabric scissors
- embroidery scissors
- tape measure
- tacking threads
- sewing needles
- beading needle

- tailor's chalk
- pins
- unpicker
- thimble
- safety pins
- fabric marker
- embroidery hoops

pre-shrinking fabric

Most fabrics you will use for making up your
projects will have been pre-shrunk by the
manufacturer. When purchasing fabric, check
this point with the retailer.

If you are not sure if a cotton or linen fabric has
been pre-shrunk, you can do this yourself before
cutting out. Soak the fabric in warm water and
then ring by hand or spin in the washing machine.
Hang the fabric outside to dry or dry it in the
tumble dryer, then remove the wrinkles by pressing
with a steam iron. The fabric is now ready to use.

measuring and cutting out

PATTERNS AND TEMPLATES

Some of the projects in this book are
accompanied by a template or pattern diagram.

The templates are reproduced on pages
107–9. Trace the template for your chosen project
onto tracing paper. Mark all seam allowances,
notches and balance marks (see page 105),
embroidery positions and so on shown on the
template onto the tracing paper version. Pin this

tracing paper template to your fabric and cut out around it. Mark the embroidery positions and any other relevant points onto the fabric using tailor's chalk, and snip all notches and balance marks before unpinning the template.

Pattern diagrams are reproduced alongside the instructions for the relevant project. Use the measurements shown on the diagram to make a pattern in tracing paper, marking in all seam allowances, notches and balance marks, and the positions of the embroidery, buttonholes and so on. Pin this tracing paper pattern to your fabric and cut out around it. Mark the embroidery and buttonhole positions, and any other relevant points, onto the fabric using tailor's chalk, and snip all notches and balance marks before unpinning the pattern.

Notches are V-shaped marks cut at right angles into the edges of paper patterns and templates, indicating seam allowances. Balance marks are cut in the same way, to ensure accurate joining of fabric pieces. Snip through the notches on paper patterns and templates, cutting into the fabric to transfer the relevant points from the pattern to the fabric. Do not cut into the fabric by more than 0.3cm (⅛in).

seams

For the neatest results, pin and tack all seams before machine stitching. Make the tacking line slightly further out towards the raw edges of the fabric than the seam line, so that the machine stitching does not have to be worked directly on top of it. Once the machine stitching is complete, remove the tacking threads.

When sewing up seams, use the reverse stitch button on your machine to secure the beginning and end of each line of stitching. Start to stitch about 1cm (⅜in) down the seam line. Reverse up to the end before stitching forwards down the seam line to the other end, then reverse back up the stitching line for 1cm (⅜in) to prevent the stitches unravelling later.

Pressing seams flat between each stage of machine stitching will make your work look much crisper. Trim the excess seam allowances to within 0.7cm (¼in) of the stitch line. Relieve any bulk at the corners by trimming across them at an angle – this will give a sharp point when it is turned to the right side.

Clip into curved seam allowances to prevent the fabric puckering and to allow it to be pressed flat when ironed. Seam allowances that lie on the inside of a curved seam should be notched to get rid of excess fabric and allow the seam to lie smoothly: cut little V shapes into the seam allowance at intervals, almost to the stitch line. Seam allowances on the outside of a curved seam should be clipped: cut into the seam allowance at intervals, at right angles and almost to the stitch line. This allows the curve of the seam allowance to spread out and releases tension in the fabric.

Secure all raw edges on seam allowances with zigzag stitch on your sewing machine, to prevent the fabric fraying.

hems

Slipstitching is a method of hemming that makes the stitching as invisible as possible. By picking up the tiniest piece of fabric with the needle from the wrong side of the fabric and sliding the needle into the folded edge of the hem, there should be almost no stitching visible on the right side.

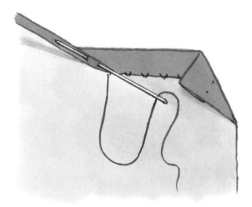

Slipstitching a hem

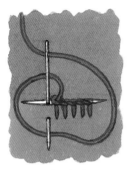

Buttonhole stitch

fastenings

BUTTONHOLES

Buttonholes can be stitched either by machine or by hand. To make machine-stitched buttonholes you will need to refer to your sewing machine manual for instructions, because each machine is slightly different.

Hand-stitched buttonholes are neatened using buttonhole stitch. Working from right to left with the point of the needle facing you, take the needle under the raw edge and up through the underside of the fabric at the required distance from the edge. Loop the thread behind both ends of the needle and pull the needle out of the fabric towards the raw edge, pulling the loop taut to cover the raw edge. Continue in this way, keeping the stitches as close together as possible, until you reach the beginning again, then secure the stitches neatly on the underside of the buttonhole.

LOOPS AND TIES

To make a tie or loop for fastening or hanging, cut a strip of fabric on the straight grain about 5cm (2in) wide and as long as you want it. When sewn, the tie or loop will be 1.3–2cm (½–¾in) wide. Fold and press the strip of fabric in half lengthways, wrong sides together. Open out the strip and turn in the long raw edges by about 1cm (⅜in) (1). Press. Fold in half again at the centre crease line, wrong sides together. Pin, tack and machine topstitch down the two folded raw edges, about 0.3cm (⅛in) in from the edge, to complete the tie (2).

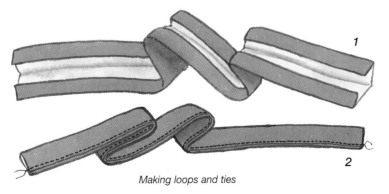

1

2

Making loops and ties

CORDS

A simple fastening can be made by threading a cord through stitched tunnelling and drawing it up tight. Attach a safety pin to one end of the cord. Push the safety pin through one hole of the tunnelling, easing the cord with it, and continue to push it through the tunnelling until the safety pin emerges from the other hole. Wrap a piece of adhesive tape around the cord at the point where you want to cut it. Cut the cord to length in the middle of the adhesive tape, peel off the tape and knot the ends of the cord. Pull the cord to close.

MOUNTING PICTURES

The Chinese Toile Sampler and Horse Picture (see pages 78 and 88) have been made up into framed pictures, but in fact many of the designs in this book would lend themselves to this treatment. You can take your finished work to a professional for framing, but it is relatively easy to frame your embroideries yourself.

Cut a piece of acid-free mounting board to the size of your picture frame and place it at the back of your embroidery. Secure the embroidery with masking tape on two facing sides. Using a large needle and strong thread, lace the fabric edges together across the back of the board with herringbone stitch. Work outwards from the middle of each side, gently pulling the stitches taut. Repeat the process for the other two sides, first tucking in the spare fabric at the corners.

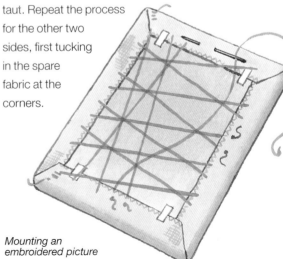

Mounting an embroidered picture

templates

Trace around the template shapes; they are the same size as the projects and include seam allowance. Pencil in the relevant markings, cut out carefully and use the pattern as instructed for each project.

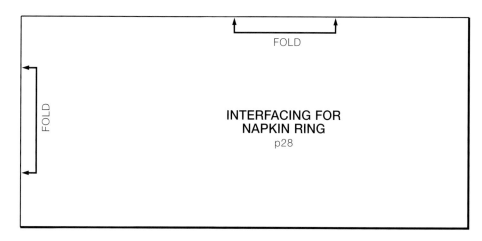

FOLD

FOLD

**INTERFACING FOR
NAPKIN RING**
p28

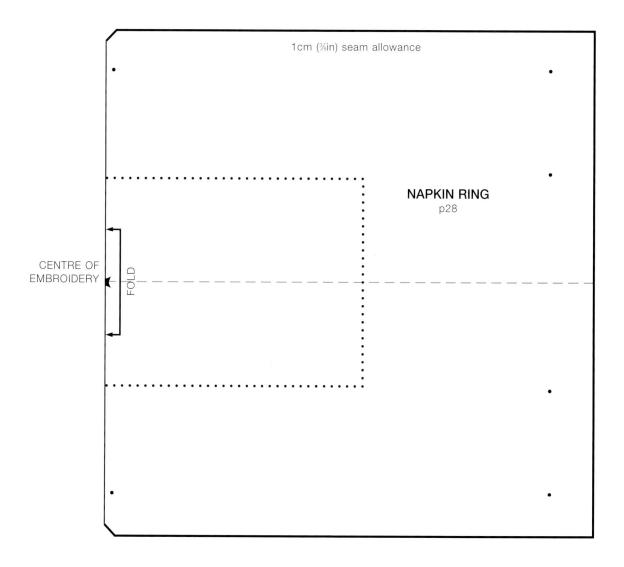

1cm (⅜in) seam allowance

NAPKIN RING
p28

CENTRE OF
EMBROIDERY

FOLD

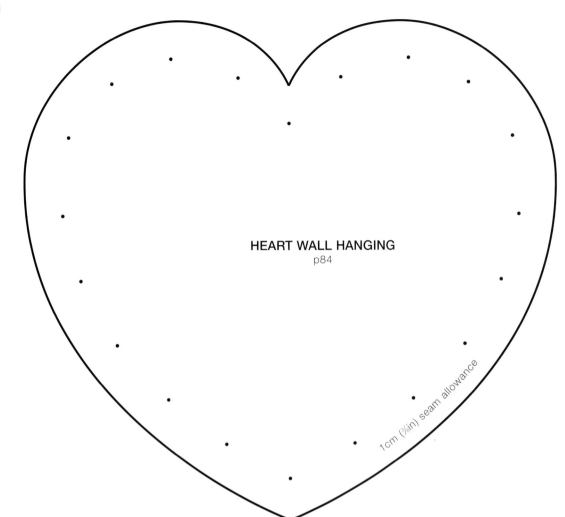

HEART WALL HANGING
p84

1cm (⅜in) seam allowance

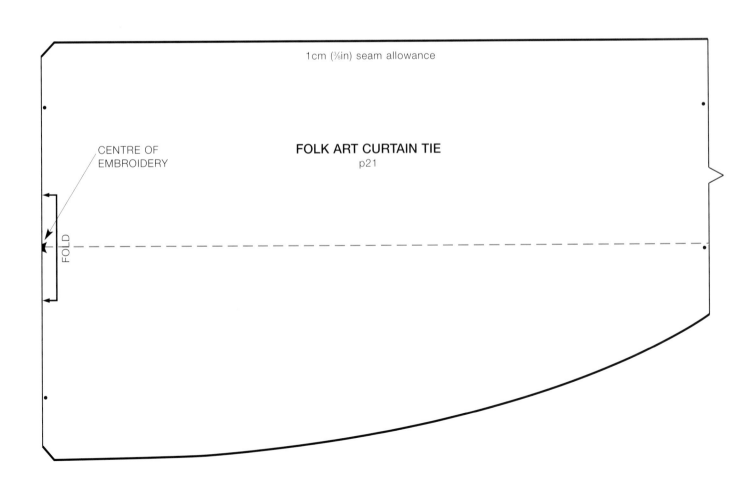

1cm (⅜in) seam allowance

CENTRE OF
EMBROIDERY

FOLD

FOLK ART CURTAIN TIE
p21

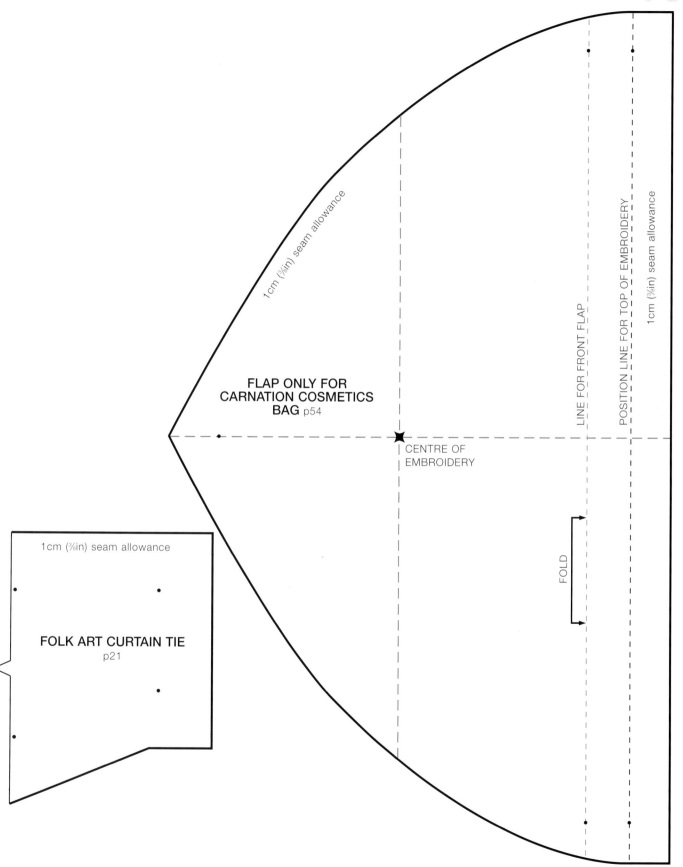

FLAP ONLY FOR
CARNATION COSMETICS
BAG p54

1cm (⅜in) seam allowance

CENTRE OF
EMBROIDERY

LINE FOR FRONT FLAP

POSITION LINE FOR TOP OF EMBROIDERY

1cm (⅜in) seam allowance

FOLD

1cm (⅜in) seam allowance

FOLK ART CURTAIN TIE
p21

index

acknowledgements

Once again a big thank you to Wendy Cockburn, who has embroidered all of the designs in this book with great care and patience.

Thank you to my friends and family – Helen, Joan, Maureen, Rosie, Ian, my mother Pepi and my father James – who have dug deep into their cupboards and pulled out all sorts of red and white objects.

Thank you to Cara Ackerman from DMC for sending me all the materials needed for all the projects. Finally, thank you to Alex, my son, for once more helping me to learn a little bit more about the computer.

Executive Editor Doreen Palamartschuk-Gillon
Editor Katy Denny
Copy-editor Sarah Widdicombe
Proofreader Bella Cunha
Executive Art Editor Peter Burt
Designer Lisa Tai
Location Photographer Paul Bricknell
Source Photographer Peter Pugh-Cook
Illustrator Kate Simunek
Chart Artwork Raymond Turvey
Picture Librarian Jennifer Veall
Production Manager Louise Hall
Senior Production Controller Jo Sim

The Publishers would like to thank those companies who generously loaned materials and props for the location photography.

pages 42/56
Jane Churchill Fabrics, national stockists 020 8877 6400

page 62
Colefax and Fowler, national stockists 020 8877 6400

pages 2/6/8
Copyright © Laura Ashley Limited 2001

pages 6/98
Kenneth Clark Ceramics, telephone 01273 476761